HOW TO PLAY
BASS GUITAR IN 50 SONGS
MODULE 1

ISBN NO: 978-1-9196519-5-8

HOW TO PLAY BASS DOT COM LTD

Copyright 2021 by Paul Wolfe
All Rights Reserved

No part of this publication may be reproduced in any form or by any means without the prior written permission of the author and/or publisher

www.how-to-play-bass.com

Author Photo copyright Julie Kaye Photography

Dedicated to Matilda Moon!

Table Of Contents

How To Use This Book.. 6

Module 1.1 The Two Finger Rest Stroke.. 8

Module 1.2 Plucking Hand 1... 13

Module 1.3 Plucking Hand 2... 16

Module 1.4 Plucking Hand 3... 21

Module 1.5 Plucking Hand 4... 24

Module 1.6 Fretting Hand - Double Bass Fingering.................................... 29

Module 1.7 Fretting Hand - One Finger Per Fret... 31

Module 1.8 What Is An 80-20 Bass Device?.. 33

Module 1.9 Device 1 The Root Note... 35

Module 1.10 Song#1 "Don't Imagine"... 39

Module 1.11 Plucking Hand 5... 43

Module 1.12 Plucking Hand 6... 48

Module 1.13 Plucking Hand 7... 53

Module 1.14 Plucking Hand 8... 58

Module 1.15 Song#2 "Have I Told You Recently"....................................... 62

Module 1.16 Plucking Hand 9... 65

Module 1.17 Song#3 "Hey John".. 70

Module 1.18 Plucking Hand 10... 73

Module 1.19 Song #4 "Every Country Breath You Take"	78
Module 1.20 Plucking Hand 11	81
Module 1.21 Device 2 - The 5th	86
Module 1.22 Fretboard Mastery 1	90
Module 1.23 Plucking Hand 12	93
Module 1.24 Fretting Hand 3	98
Module 1.25 Fretting Hand 4	101
Module 1.26 Fretboard Mastery 2	107
Module 1.27 More Practice With The 5th	110
Module 1.28 Song#5 "Bad Mooon Falling"	117
Module 1.29 Quarter Notes With Rests	121
Module 1.30 Fretboard Mastery 3	127
Module 1.31 Song #6 "Love Me Don't"	130
Module 1.32 Song#7 "Blue River"	134
Module 1.33 Fretboard Mastery 4	140
Module 1.34 Country Two Beat Blues	141
Module 1.35 Creating A Dynamic Practice Schedule	145
Module 1.36 Module 1 Checklist And Guidelines	155

Thanks

As always, the writing of this book was made easier (and better) by having the watchful eyes and assistance of a group of beta students. Thanks to each and every one of them:

- Tyrone Aaron
- David Overton
- Colin Baxter
- James Glen
- Vincent Niklaus
- Steve Vinoski
- Carl Beesley
- Donna Eyman
- Wayne Pederson
- Pierre Sonigo
- Ron Kramer
- Rob March
- Jason Anderson
- Greg Chaseling
- David Leigh
- Richard Rosenbloom
- Alan Philpotts
- Thomas Nelson
- Nick Hardesty
- Daniel Picard
- Robert Bonitz
- Brett Helmreich
- Michel Doiron
- Tony Mortillaro
- William Sederholm
- David Price
- William Avery
- Jack Nash
- John Curry
- Kit Koger
- Gerry Jormby
- Joe Sokohl
- Robert Cecchini
- Jeffrey Siegel
- Andy Roberts
- Arthur Forgie
- Pete McCormick
- Einar Sorensen
- Birger Malstrom
- Ben Greer
- Axel Knudsen
- Thomas Tofexis
- Manny Linares
- Patrick Boassy
- Robert Zimmer
- David Highton
- Joe Fichera
- Andre Fischer
- Josh Knisley
- Jón Eyjólfsson
- Leslie Zigel
- Karen McIntyre
- Chuck Lazer
- John Willoughby
- Greg Jackson
- Willie Munt
- Richard Wilde
- Terry McCormick
- Patricia Dallam
- Wendall Goff

Online Version Of This Book (Plus Bonuses)

The printed copy of this volume is designed to be used with the online version. If you purchased your printed copy from Amazon, then all you have to do to get access to the online version is send an email with a copy of your Amazon receipt or invoice to me at this address:

paul@how-to-play-bass.com

I'll add you to the online version of the book and email you a link to log in. As well as the videos of the majority of the musical examples, you can also download MP3 practice tracks from the online version of the book. There are also some extended lessons and bonus lessons too.

The majority of the music examples in the book are filmed so you can see and hear how each of the examples is played and sounds. The filmed examples are edited with picture in picture technology, so you can see fretting hand and plucking hand close up. Here's a screenshot showing what that looks like:

Each section of the book has a corresponding section in the online version so you can quickly find the video examples as you're reading or working through this volume.

How To Use This Book

This is the first book in a series of five. As noted on the Amazon description page for this Volume, this is a detailed and sequential course that requires disciplined and focused practice over time in order to get the results on the bass guitar that you want.

ASSUMPTIONS

The remaining four volumes of this series will follow on naturally from this volume. But this volume has to start somewhere, so the following assumptions have been made:

- You have a bass guitar and know that the four strings are E, A, D and G from lowest pitched to highest. The E string is the thickest. The G string is the thinnest.

- You have some kind of tuner, and know how to tune the strings.

- You understand tab. Every musical example is presented in notation and tab, and has an accompanying video in the online version (filmed at two tempos) so you can see and hear how each example should be played. The combination of videos and tab in for each exampleallows you to play the example.

- You have a smart device or computer or MP3 player so that you can use the MP3 practice tracks that are found on the various unit pages of the online version of the book.

If any of the first three is an issue for you, let me know and I'll point you in the direction of some resources on them - or create some myself.

Each unit in the book is designed to be a self contained lesson. The last section of the book serves as both a checklist and a guide to the tempo level you should strive to acquire before you can consider each unit thoroughly learned.

Some units may take several days to work through, and some may take just one or two practice sessions. One thing to note: there's a degree of overlap in several of the units so that your practice schedule can incorporate more than one unit in a practice session.

For example, in your early practice you could be working on the exercises from Plucking Hand 4, the double bass fingering lesson, the one finger per fret lesson and Module 1.9 with the root note exercises all in one practice session.

Creating A Practice Schedule

Long term success - as defined by making improvements on the bass - requires two things:

- A sequential learning system.

- Creating a disciplined approach to working through the learning system that involves planning what you are going to practice, tracking your practice, reviewing and auditing your practice at regular intervals.

My sequential learning system for the bass guitar is covered in the five volumes of this series. My approach to practice is covered more fully in **Deliberate Practice For Bass Guitar** and **The 12 Week Practice Cycle For Bass Guitar,** but I've added a section to the end of the book on setting up a practice system that you should read in order to make your practice as efficient as possible.

Even if you've only got 15 or 20 minutes a day to practice, provided you are organized before you start, focused during each of those short practice sessions, and periodically review what you're practicing you can still make progress.

15 minutes of focused practice consistently done always beats hours spent on random practice. Always.

One final thing before you get started...most methods teach what you should do. But there are common mistakes that every student makes that are worth being made aware of. There is a bonus lesson in the online version called COMMON MISTAKES. There are four common mistakes detailed on that video that are worth checking from time to time to see if these are cropping up in your playing.

Module 1.1 - Introducing The Two Finger Rest Stroke

There are several different ways of sounding the bass with the plucking hand: the two finger rest stroke; one finger rest stroke; three or four finger styles; slapping; tapping; playing with a pick; thumb and palm mute; thumb and index/ring fingers (classical guitar style).

Bass players who have graduated to intermediate level may know several of these different plucking styles and have them in their tool boxes to use for different playing situations.

As a beginner, you need a foundational plucking hand technique which will stand you in good stead for the majority of your playing. When you're getting started out, you need to focus on just one plucking hand style and develop that plucking hand style.

The plucking hand style that I recommend is the Two Finger Rest Stroke. This plucking hand style is named because it uses two fingers of your plucking hand - the index and the middle fingers - and because when you play on a higher string you play 'through' that string and come to rest on the string below. (More on this in a moment.)

Why The Two Finger Rest Stroke?

There are several reasons why I teach the two finger rest stroke:

#1 The first reason is to do with fingers versus pick (or plectrum). Finger playing gives a rounder, fuller sound than playing with a pick and in my opinion is usable in more situations than playing with a pick.

That doesn't mean playing with a pick *isn't* something you should aspire to in the future. But a good, two finger technique, is more versatile for beginners than playing with a pick.

#2 The two finger rest stroke gives you a good combination of speed and dexterity. There are notable 'two finger' players who played fast enough for most musical situations (e.g. Jaco Pastorius and Rocco Prestia).

#3 While three and four finger plucking hand styles are used by advanced players - name players like rock monster Billy Sheehan, jazz fusion maestro Steve Bailey and jazzers like Janek Gwizdala, Gary Willis and Matt Garrison - these players have created their own idiosyncratic plucking hand styles that serve their musical visions. If you get to the stage where two finger rest stroke doesn't support your musical vision.... then there are alternative models that you can check out to improve speed and dexterity.

But do note that speed is not everything - and that for 99% of playing situations a good, solid two finger rest stroke technique is more than adequate.

#4. Styles like slapping, tapping, thumb and palm mute and so on, give different tonal sounds to your playing toolbox. But there are very few gig situations where one of these styles *on its own* will get you through.

Introduction To The Two Finger Rest Stroke

Here are the important elements of the Two Finger Rest Stroke:

- You'll use the index and middle fingers of your plucking hand to pluck the strings. As a rule of thumb when you are playing in an ascending manner you alternate picking with these fingers but when you are playing in a descending manner you lead with the finger that plucked the string above.

- When you pluck a higher string, your finger plucks through that string and comes to 'rest' on the string below. Hence the name 'rest' stroke. So if you were plucking the G string, your plucking finger would come to rest on the D string. If you were plucking the D string, your finger would come to rest on the A string. And if you were plucking the A string, your finger would come to rest on the E string.

- This 'rest stroke' serves two purposes: it helps ensure even picking because your fingers travel approximately the same distance when plucking any string; when combined with the location of the thumb the rest stroke helps mute strings and stop unwanted strings sounding out.

- Your thumb moves depending on which string you are playing and mutes strings that are not being played.

The Three Thumb Positions In Two Finger Rest Stroke

(i) When you are playing on the E string the thumb rests on the corner of the pick up. Like this:

(ii) When you are playing on the A string the thumb rests on the top of the E string. Like this:

(iii) When you are playing on the D or G strings, the thumb rests on the top of the A string *and*, the side of the thumb makes light contact with the E string (so muting it). Like this:

We'll start practicing the two finger rest stroke shortly. This unit is laying the foundation for the two finger rest stroke .It also provides a reference that you can come back to at any time and and review the foundations.

One Final Thing To Note

There's one other part of plucking hand technique that is fundamental - and that's the position of the arm. Here's a screenshot showing this:

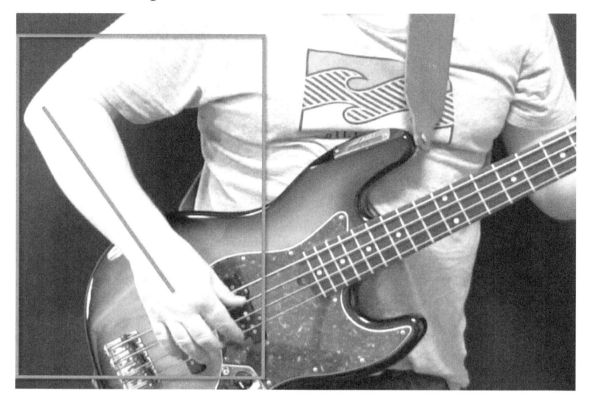

The issue here is the angle of the wrist. I've seen many bass players rest the underside of their forearms on the body of their bass and then crook their wrist so that their fingers can play the bass.

The reason this is an issue is that all the tendons that operate the fingers run in a straight line to the elbow.

If you play with your wrist bent then what you're doing is reducing your potential efficiency because you are stretching the tendons. Playing like this can also contribute to issues like repetitive strain injuries. So it's important to remember your arm position and try to get it as straight as possible.

Module 1.2 Plucking Hand 1

Pre-Lesson Content

On the online version of this Unit is some pre-lesson exercises for you to do if you are new to counting whole notes. If you can already count whole notes comfortably, then proceed with the lesson.

Playing Whole Notes On The Bass With The Two Fingered Rest Stroke

The first two fingered rest stroke exercise involves the open E string played in whole notes. Like this:

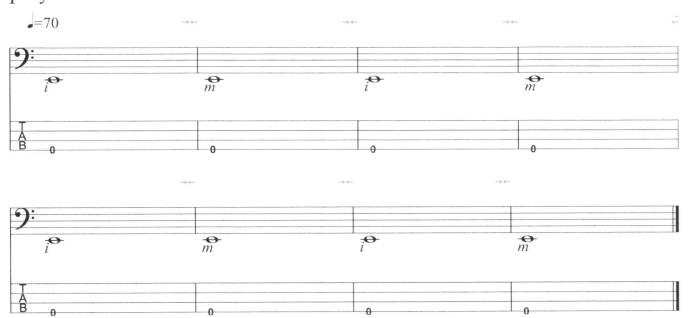

Some things to note:

- I've added additional notation under the notes. Either an 'i' or an 'm.' These notations stand for 'index' and 'middle' and refer to the fingers of the plucking hand to use.

- When playing the two finger rest stroke there are 'guidelines' to follow. The first one is, if playing on the same string, then you strictly alternate fingers.

- The second guideline for this exercise is that you are playing the open E string, so the thumb should be anchored on the corner of a pickup

- I added some notations in the first and last bars - at the start there is something that looks a little like this: ||: And at the end of the last bar it's like this: :||

- These are called START and END repeat bars and are an instruction to repeat everything between them.

- Although I've filmed this at 70 BPM as indicated on the top left on the notation/tab above - you can start at 60 BPM. And obviously you can work through the different tempo drum tracks that I've provided.

The next exercise is identical to the previous exercise, but this time you pluck the first note with the middle finger and your strict alternation of middle finger to index finger starts with the first note:

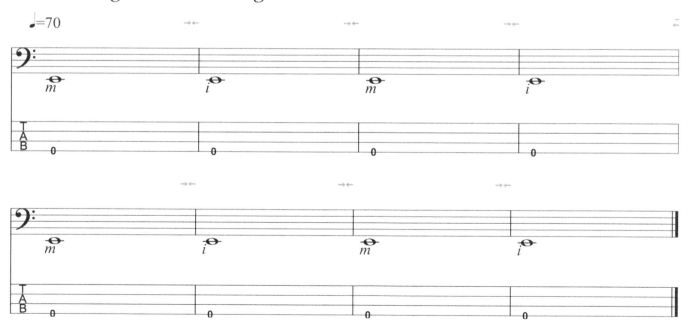

14   Module 1.2

Action Steps For Module 1.2

Most units have a series of action steps to go through to guide your practice.

1. Download the Whole Note drum tracks. These are in a zipped file and exist at different tempos (60, 70, 80, 90, 100 BPM) and at different bar lengths (8 bars, 16 bars and 32 bars).

2. Spend time counting through the drum grooves and being able to synchronize your '1-2-3-4' count with the drum hits.

3. Spend time counting through the drum tracks and maintain the count but tap your plucking hand. A table top. Your thigh. Wherever.

4. Now play through with the drum tracks playing the open E string and using the alternating fingers. Focus on ensuring you are alternating your index and middle finger - and focus on alternating which finger you start with.

5. Don't be in a hurry to move through the tempo levels. Instead be in a 'hurry' to feel totally comfortable and relaxed when you play the open string whole notes *and* count through the bars.

Practice Tracks For Module 1.2

Practice tracks can be downloaded from the online version of this unit.

Module 1.3 - Plucking Hand 2

In this unit we're going to apply the two finger rest stroke to the other three open strings. Just like the exercises in Module 1.2, separate exercises leading with both the index finger and the middle finger will be applied to the other three open strings.

Two more elements of the two finger rest stroke to focus on in this module are the position of your plucking hand thumb for each exercise, and ensuring your plucking hand finger plays through the string and comes to 'rest' on the string below.

The Two Finger Rest Stroke With The A String

When playing on the A string, the thumb should be positioned on the E string and the plucking hand finger should pluck through the A string to rest on the E string. Here's the exercise leading with the index finger:

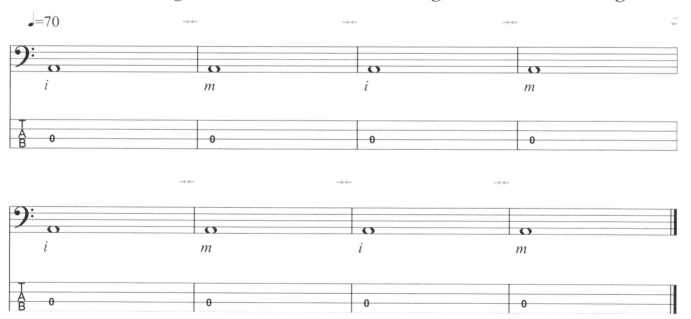

Here's the exercise leading with the middle finger:

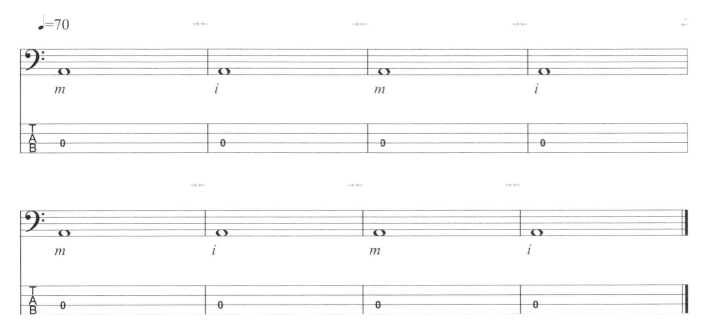

One other thing to note: if you check the videos of the examples you'll see that, when I start any of the exercises. the finger that I am going to lead with is in position and poised to play the string before I start playing it. And my fingers then go through a slow, walking kind of motion, so the next finger that is going to be used to play is getting into position before it's required.

The Two Finger Rest Stroke With The D String

Here's the exercise leading with the index finger but this time plucking the open D string. The thumb moves to the top of the A string, and the side of the thumb remains in contact with the E string, and the plucking hand finger plucks through the D string to rest on the A string:

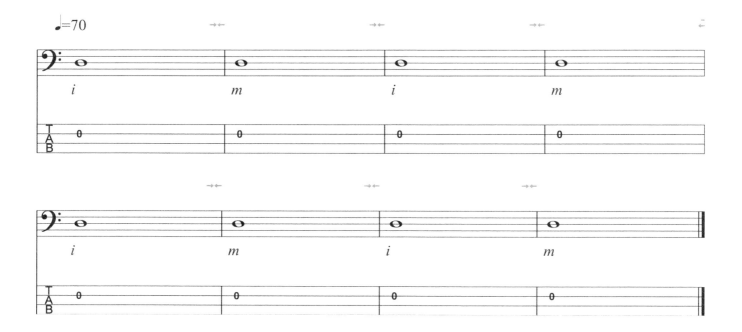

Here's the exercise on the open D string leading with the middle finger:

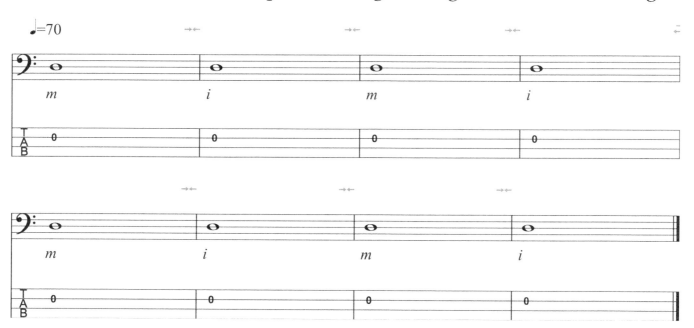

The Two Finger Rest Stroke With The G String

Here's the exercise leading with the index finger on the open G string - the thumb remains positioned on the A string, and the plucking finger plucks through the G string and comes to rest on the D string:

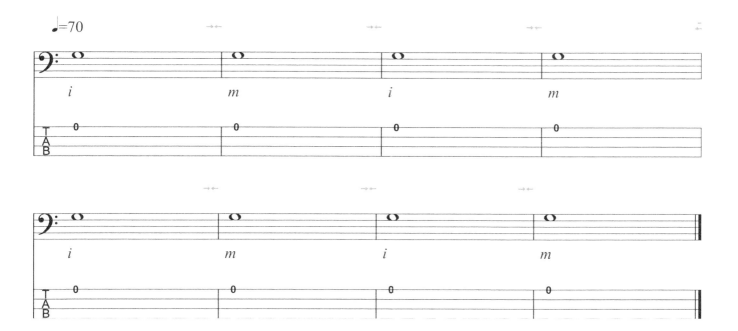

Here's the exercise on the open G string leading with the middle finger:

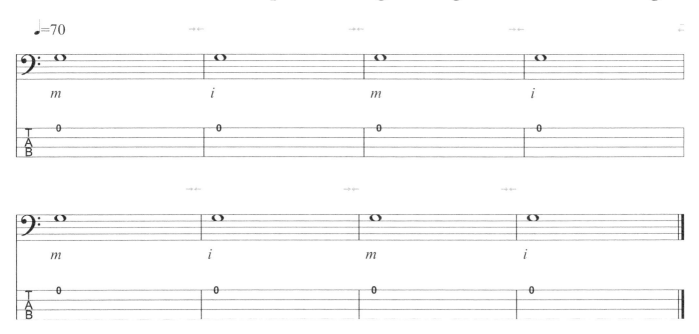

Action Steps

1. Select a practice track tempo that you are comfortable with from the practice tracks that you downloaded from the Module 1.2 page.

2. Start with the A string and play through the whole note exercise. Don't forget to alternate starting with either index or middle finger and don't forget to position your thumb in the correct location. If you feel comfortable at the tempo level you are working on, then try the next tempo level.

3. Repeat the exercise with the open D and the open G strings in turn. Pay attention to having your thumb in the correct location for each string as well as alternating exercises starting with either index or middle finger.

Don't forget to play through the string and come to 'rest' on the string below.

Module 1.4 Plucking Hand 3

Pre-Lesson Content

There are pre-lesson exercises for you to do if you are new to counting half notes on the online Module 1.4 page. If you can already count half notes comfortably, then proceed with the lesson.

Playing Half Notes On The Bass With The Two Fingered Rest Stroke

In this unit we're going to combine playing on the open E string with the two fingered rest stroke and playing in a half note rhythm. Here's the first exercise:

- Remember the first guideline with Two Finger Rest Stroke: when playing on the same string that you strictly alternate fingers.

- The second guideline for this exercise is that you are playing the open E string, so the thumb should be anchored on the corner of a pickup

- Although I've filmed this at 80 BPM as indicated by the tempo marking on the top left on the notation/tab above – you can start at 60 BPM. And obviously you can work through the different tempo drum tracks that I've provided.

As with the examples in Module 1.2, we're going to practice the same example but start by plucking the first note with the middle finger:

The reason we practice leading with either finger is that when we start crossing strings in a descending fashion, the alternation rules change, there are playing situations where which finger you need to 'lead' with changes.

Action Steps

1. Download the half note drum tracks from the online Module page. These are in a zipped file and exist at different tempos (60, 70, 80, 90, 100 BPM) and at different bar lengths (8 bars, 16 bars and 32 bars).

2. Spend time counting through the drum grooves and being able to synchronize your '1-2-3-4' count with the drum hits.

3. Spend time counting through the drum grooves and maintain the count but tap your plucking hand somewhere on the appropriate beats. A table top. Your thigh. Wherever.

4. Now play through the exercises playing the open E string and using the alternating fingers. Focus on ensuring you are alternating your index and middle finger – and focus on alternate which finger you start with.

5. Don't be in a hurry to move through the tempo levels. Instead focus on feeling comfortable and relaxed when you play the open string half notes AND count through the bars.

Module 1.5 - Plucking Hand 4

In this unit we're going to practice the two finger rest stroke with the remaining open strings.

The Two Finger Rest Stroke With The A String/Half Note Rhythm

Here's the exercise leading with the index finger - remember to concentrate on the alternation of the plucking hand fingers, positioning the thumb on the top of the E string, and that the plucking hand finger plucks through the A string and comes to 'rest' on the E string:

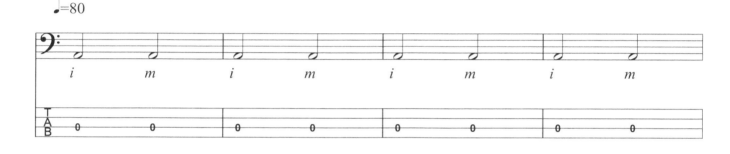

Here's the exercise leading with the middle finger:

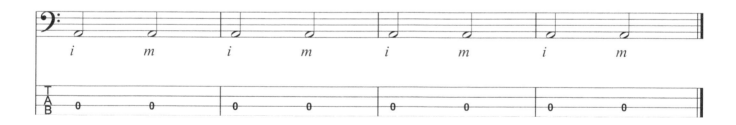

One other thing to note: if you check these plucking hand videos that you'll see that when I start any of the exercises the finger that I am going to lead with is in position and poised to play the string *before* I start playing it. And my fingers then go through a slow, walking kind of motion so the next finger that is going to pluck is getting into position *before* the next stroke.

The Two Finger Rest Stroke With The D String/Half Note Rhythm

Here's the exercise leading with the index finger but this time plucking the open D string - remember to concentrate on the alternation of the plucking hand fingers, positioning the thumb on the top of the A string, and that the plucking hand finger plucks through the D string and comes to 'rest' on the A string:

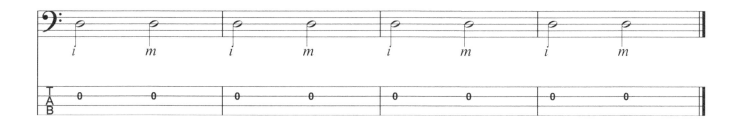

Here's the exercise on the open D string leading with the middle finger:

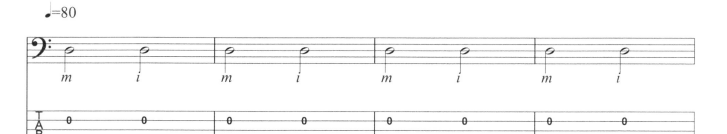

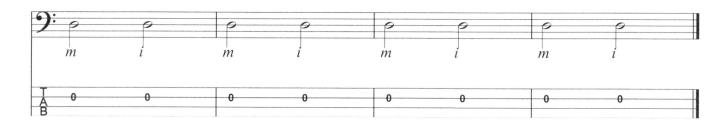

The Two Finger Rest Stroke With The G String/Half Note Rhythm

Here's the exercise leading with the index finger on the open G string - remember to concentrate on the alternation of the plucking hand fingers, the thumb remains on the top of the A string, and that the plucking hand finger plucks through the G string and comes to 'rest' on the D string:

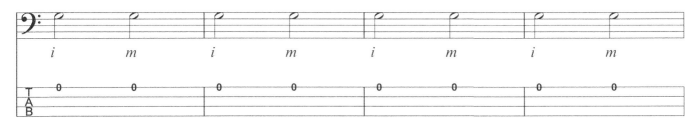

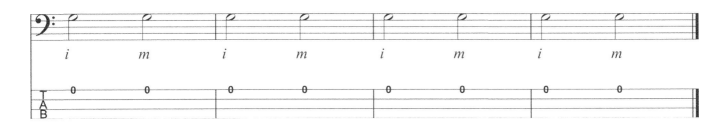

Here's the exercise on the open G string leading with the middle finger:

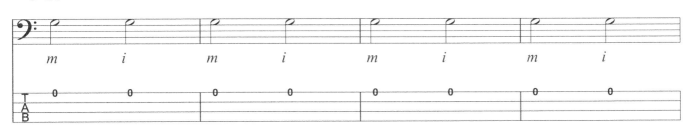

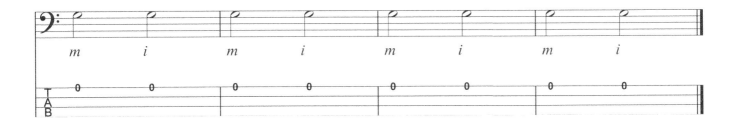

Action Steps

1. Select a practice track tempo that you are comfortable with from the practice tracks that you downloaded from the Module 1.4 page.

2. Start with the A string and play through the exercise using half notes. Don't forget to alternate starting with index or middle finger. If you feel comfortable at the tempo level you are working on, then try the next tempo level. Don't forget the position of the thumb and plucking through the string to rest on the E string below.

3. Repeat the exercise with the open D and the open G strings in turn. Remember to alternate starting with either the middle finger or the index finger. For both these exercises the thumb is positioned on the A string. Don't forget the plucking finger plays through the string and comes to rest on the string below (either the D string or the A string).

Module 1.6 Fretting Hand 1 - Double Bass Fingering

There are two videos on the online Module 1.6 page that you need to watch for this unit.

Here's the exercise you need to practice for the double bass fingering system:

Some notes:

1. I've put this exercise starting at D at the 5th fret of the A string. You can do this higher up the neck if you like and start at say F at the 8th fret of the A string. The main criteria is that it's comfortable for your fretting hand.

2. I've marked the tempo of the exercise as 60 BPM.

3. I've also marked in the finger you should fret with under each note. So you'll see this is 1-2-4-2 in terms of which fingers you fret with.

4. All the fretting hand criteria apply:

- Your fingertips should fret the note.

- You should try and move ONLY the finger that is needed to execute the next fretting position.

- When you fret with a 'higher number' finger (e.g. the 2nd finger), the lower number finger should remain in position (e.g. the 1st finger). When you fret with the 4th finger, the 1st, 2nd and 3rd fingers should all make contact with the string too.

- Keep the fingertips of the fretting hand as close to the string as possible. And so on.

- Review the videos on the lesson page for more detail.

5. I put in a repeat of the second finger as a natural lead back to the start of the exercise – and to make the exercise fit into a 4 bar pattern.

6. The note at the 6th fret of the A string is a D# *and* an Eb! Two notes that have the same pitch are called enharmonic equivalents. Other notes like this are C# and Db. Or F# and Gb. It's not anything you need to work on – but just a piece of musical information you need to be aware of.

Module 1.7 Fretting Hand 2 - One Finger Per Fret

There are two videos on the online Module 1.7 page that you need to watch for this unit.

Here's the exercise you need to practice for the one finger per fret fingering system:

Some notes:

1. I've put this exercise starting at D at the 5th fret of the A string. You can do this higher up the neck if you like and start at say F at the 8th fret of the A string. The main criteria is that it's comfortable for your hand.

2. I've marked the tempo of the exercise as 60 BPM.

3. I've also marked in the finger you should fret with under each note. So you'll see this is 1-2-3-4 in terms of which fingers you fret with.

4. All the fretting hand criteria apply:

- Your fingertips should fret the note.

- You should try and move ONLY the finger that is needed to execute the next fretting position.

- When you fret with a 'higher number' finger (e.g. the 2nd finger), the lower number finger should remain in position (e.g. the 1st finger). When you fret with the 4th finger, the 1st, 2nd and 3rd fingers should all make contact with the string too.

- Keep the fingertips of the fretting hand as close to the string as possible.

Review the videos on the lesson page for more detail.

Module 1.8 What Is An 80-20 Bass Device

Over the last ten years I've transcribed and analyzed the bass lines to over 1000 songs. That includs bass lines by James Jamerson, Paul McCartney, Tommy Shannon, Bruce Thomas, Duck Dunn, John Paul Jones, Jerry Jemmott, Rocco Prestia, Pino Palladino and dozens of others.

What I found was this:

- There are a relatively small number of ideas that crop up in the bass lines of all of these players. I call these ideas 80-20 Bass Devices. Or devices for short.

- Despite these ideas being used by all the players mentioned, and all the players we admire, I've never seen them taught. It's as if the pros know the secrets, but don't want to share them.

- Despite there being a relatively small number of devices - much less than you'd think - there are an almost infinite way that you can combine them. Especially when you use secondary ideas like modifying devices and connecting devices.

- The biggest difference between genres isn't what devices are being used, it's the rhythms being used to play them.

Over the five modules in this course we're going to learn and practice the first 10 devices. These are foundational, but will still allow you to create interesting bass lines.

For example, on the next page is an 8 bar line with a chord progression that we'll be meeting in one of the songs in the course - Blue Sugar. The full song is based on a chord progression from a commonly played Rolling Stones tune. This line uses devices and rhythms that we'll be covering over the 5 modules of this course and is the verse only:

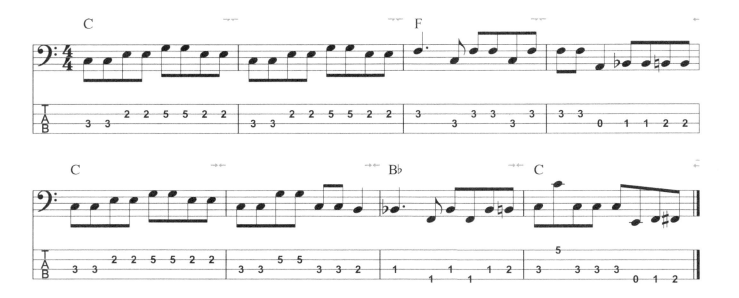

Here are the reasons identifying and knowing the 80-20 Devices is so important:

- Allows us to 'codify' each device so that when we see/hear it again we can quickly identify it.

- Allows us to isolate the device and practice it in multiple chord settings and key centres so that we become fluent with that device and can use it in our playing. That playing is either learning someone else's lines or creating our own lines.

- By identifying, isolating and practice the devices, they become part of our playing vocabulary going forward.

The first device that we're going to look at is the simplest to understand. It's the root note. And that's covered in the next Unit.

Module 1.9 Device 1 - The Root Note

The root note is the most basic device in the 80-20 Bass Vocabulary. Here's an 8 bar chord progression of C to Am7 to F to G7, which is a common chord progression found throughout rock and pop:

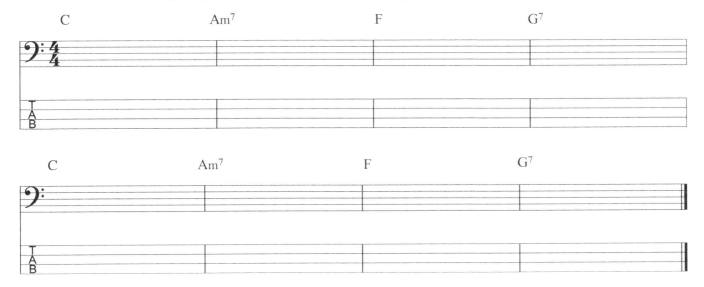

The root note for each chord - which you probably know - is simply the note name in the chord. So for the chord of C, the root note is C. For the chord of Am7, the root note is A. For the chord of F, the root note is F. And for the chord of G7, the root note is G.

Just by playing the appropriate root notes with a half note rhythm will give us a workable - if simple (and relatively static) bass line:

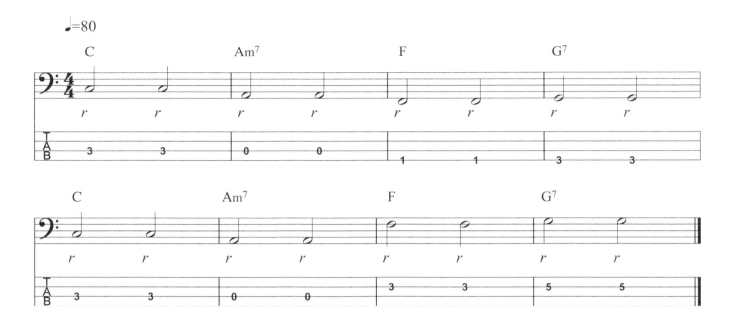

Underneath each note I've added the annotation 'r' to emphasize that the note being played is the root note. Depending on where you are in your bass journey, you may know where to find the locations of notes like C and A and F and G. If you don't, then the series of Fretboard Mastery lessons that start at Module 1.22 will help you with that. The note locations for these notes can also be found by using the tab in the example above.

There are practice tracks available to download from the online Module 1.9 page so that you can play through this example yourself.

And just to give you a foretaste of where this course will take you, here's a faster version of the same chord progression - this time played at 120 BPM - and this bass line is in 8th notes. But it's still using just root notes:

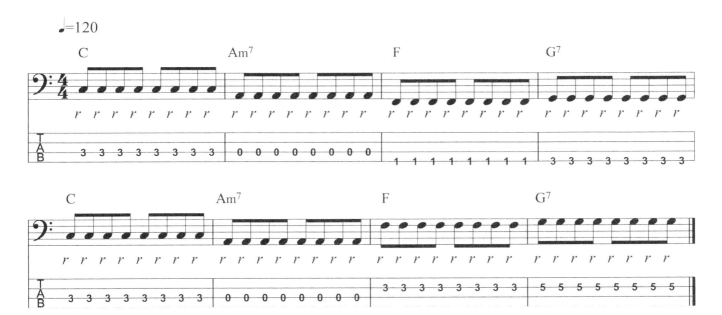

Here's another bass line example for you to practice using a half note rhythm and root notes. This chord progression is the 12 bar blues. Here's what the example looks and sounds like:

Module 1.9 37

The blues progression is common chord progression 1, and, as with the previous example, there are practice tracks at different tempo levels to download on the online Module 1.9 page so that you can learn and practice this example.

By working on both of these examples you are now practicing the following:

- Half note rhythms in a more realistic setting.

- Plucking hand and fretting hand technique with a real world chord progression.

- Playing on different notes. As noted, if you are not familiar with the note locations on the fretboard, then use the tab locations in the example.

Although root notes are the most basic device out of the 10 devices that we're going to cover over the five Modules of this program, they make a useful starting point as the 'theory' of root names is straight forward to understand. When we add in more complex rhythms in later modules, a good way to start practicing these rhythms is to combine them with real world chord progressions and root notes.

In the next unit we're going to look at the first practice song - Song #1 -which uses root notes.

Module 1.10 Song 1 - "Don't Imagine"

The practice songs that we're going to learn in How To Play Bass In 50 Songs are based on real world songs, but are adapted for the learning requirements of the course, and where you are in the course at any time.

"Don't Imagine" is a simple rock ballad that has a Verse-Chorus-Bridge format that's repeated twice. The bass line uses just root notes and either whole note or half notes as the rhythmic unit.

All of the songs in the How To Play Bass In 50 Songs follow a similar teaching approach:

- The song is 'chunked down' into its constituent parts.

- Those parts are then presented in notation and tab.

- Each of the separate sections of the song are filmed with two 'picture in picture' playalongs. The first playalong will be at performance tempo with a "band style" backing track, and the second playalong will be slower, with a chordal metronome.

- There will be practice tracks for each section that you can use to play each song chunk in isolation.

Here's how I recommend learning the different parts of the songs:

- Focus on the first part of the tune - in Song 1 it's Verse 1. Start by watching the playalong version of the video lesson. Listen to both tempo versions of the song. This is so your brain, and your ear, can start 'learning' the sound of the bass line.

- Look at the notation and tab. The chords are on the score too, so you can use the tab locations to find the notes and also know the note names. Start finding the notes and walking slowly through them. In this instance, there are only two notes to learn for the entire verse: C and F.

- There is a downloadable practice track with chordal metronome for the verse. Set that playing and see if you can play along.

- If you play through successfully, then repeat two or three times before proceeding to play with the 80 BPM track.

If you *don't* play through successfully, then:

- Think back to identify where you made an error. Correcting errors now is much easier than when you've worked something up to speed. And as a generalization, the more complex the bass line, the more exponential this becomes. As a second generalization learning something correctly the first time takes anywhere between 25 to 75% less time than learning something incorrectly and then having to go back and fix it at a later date.

- If there was a particular sequence of notes that tripped you up, then practice that sequence slowly and out of tempo several times to ensure that when you next attempt the particular song chunk with a practice track, you have a high chance of successfully playing through that section.

- When you are happy with a section at a specific tempo then move onto the next section. And repeat the process.

- There are only really three chunks in this song - the verse, chorus and bridge - then when you have mastered these you can try putting them together to play the complete practice song.

Let's go through the song sections one at a time. First up is the verse and this uses only two root notes (as there are only two chords) and uses a whole note rhythm:

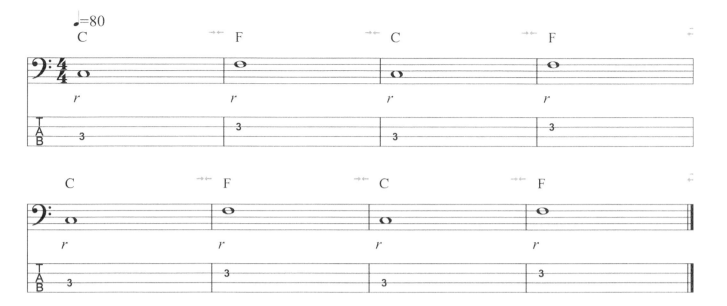

The chorus is a 4 bar section that mixes half note and whole note rhythms. There are also some chords known as 'slash chords.' These are Am/E and F/C. Without getting bogged down in theory when you see a slash chord the bass plays the note on the right of the slash chord. So for Am/E, the bass plays E. And for F/C, the bass plays C. Here's the chorus:

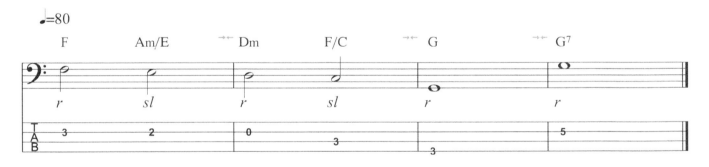

Finally there's an 8 bar bridge section. This is in a half note rhythm throughout the section except for the last bar of the section which is a whole note:

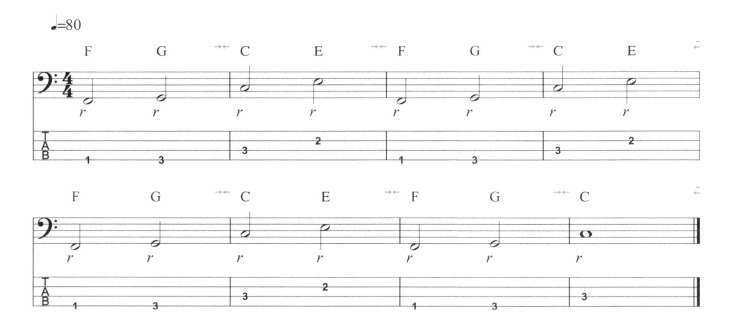

On the website version of Module 1.10 you'll find a PDF with the song sections arranged together that you can print out and put on your music stand. Additionally there are playalongs of the complete song at different tempo levels, which puts the song sections together like this:

- Verse
- Chorus
- Bridge
- Verse
- Chorus
- Bridge
- Song finishes with a C chord, so play a C to finish.

Module 1.11 Plucking Hand 5 - Cross String Plucking

So far we've been dealing with single string playing - and either leading with the index finger or middle finger, and then strictly alternating the two plucking fingers used. You may have noticed when learning Song#1 in the previous unit that the plucking hand exercises already practiced don't prepare the plucking hand for playing notes on different strings. That's what we're going to work on in the next four units.

When plucking across strings, there are further guidelines for the Two Finger Rest Stroke to start working on:

- When playing on the same string - or ascending strings - the strict two finger alternation is used.

- When descending strings - e.g. going from the A string to the E string - we use 'raking' and lead with the finger that played the prior string.

Additionally we have to incorporate the movement of the thumb into these exercises as well, as its position is determined by what string you are plucking.

So we're going to work through a series of exercises starting with the E string and the A string to start training our plucking hands to do this. Slow and perfect repetitions of these exercises are vital to train our brains to 'automate' this crucial part of plucking hand technique.

Exercise 1 and 2 - Ascending Only, E String to A string - Whole Notes

In Exercise 1 we are going to play an 8 bar exercise and play four bars of open E strings and then four bars of open A strings. Here's what the exercise looks like:

Things to note:

(i) As always the tempo is just a guideline. I've got 70 BPM notated at the top of the score...if you have to start at 60 BPM or slower then do so. Slow and perfect ALWAYS trumps faster and imperfect.

(ii) The exercise is ONLY 8 bars long. It is important that you don't play the exercise with a longer drum beat. (You'll see why in a moment.)

(iii) If you've been through and mastered prior modules the *only* point where this exercise should be challenging and/or different is going from bar 4 to bar 5 where you move from the open E string to the open A string.

(iv) If need be, practice that movement of the thumb from the pick up/thumb rest to the open A string out of tempo and in isolation from the rest of the exercise. (In fact, this is a good preparation for this exercise).

When you're comfortable - and the audit point to watch for to know you are feeling comfortable is the transition from the E string to the A string - then reverse which finger you lead with and play this variation of the exercise:

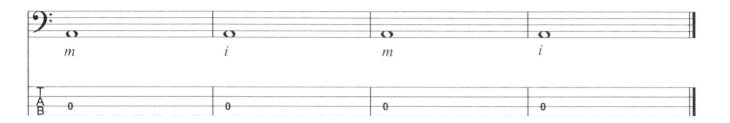

Exercise 3 and 4 - Starting With The Rest Stroke - A String To E String

Now we're going to incorporate the rest stroke.

In this exercise we're going to play four bars of open A strings and then four bars of open E strings. Here's the exercise:

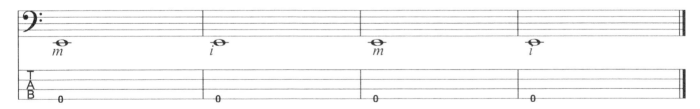

In this exercise the placement of the thumb and its subsequent movement changes. The thumb starts on the top of the E string ready for the fingers to pluck the A string.

In bar 5 the thumb moves to the top of pickup position in order to play the E string.

BUT NOTE THE 'REST STROKE.' The middle finger plucks the last A string in bar 4 - but the action of the rest stroke with the middle finger coming to rest on the E string means that it's in prime position to play the E string. So that's the finger we use to play the E string.

The remaining bars continue the guideline of strict alternation of the fingers when playing on the same string or ascending.

PLEASE RE-READ THAT AGAIN CAREFULLY AND CHECK OUT THE VIDEOS ON THE UNIT PAGE SO YOU FOLLOW THIS!

If we start playing on the A string leading with the middle finger, when we move to the E string at the end of bar 4, it will be the index finger that plucks through and 'rests' on the string below and is used in bar 5. Like this:

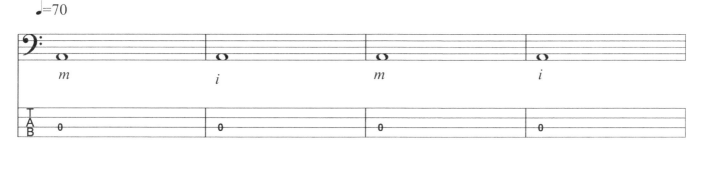

Making This A 16 Bar Exercise:

If we take both of the above examples and extend them to 16 bars by repeating the 8 bars, we get an interesting combination of both of the above exercises. For space reasons, these can be found on the online Module 1.11 page.

Action Steps

1. Select a practice track tempo that you are comfortable with from the Whole Note practice tracks in your practice library.

2. Start with Exercises 1 and 2 - which are about working on transitioning the thumb from the top of the pick up to the top of the E string as you play the open E string and open A string respectively.

3. Play that several times. Work on the movement of the thumb separately and out of tempo if you need to.

4. To avoid favouring one finger over another, make sure that you switch and practice leading with the middle finger.

5. When you are comfortable with this, then move on to Exercises 3 and 4 where you start on the A string and play to the E string. Pay careful attention to the interruption to the strict alternation caused by raking and then continue the strict alternation.

6. When you have played these exercises several times then switch to a 16 bar long track and play the final two exercises (Found on the online version of Module 1.11). Focus on plucking with the correct finger when moving from the A string to E string using the rest stroke.

Module 1.12 - Plucking Hand 6

In this unit, the same procedure from Module 1.11 will be used to work on our string crossing with the plucking hand. The difference is the rhythmic intensity of the exercises which uses the half note rhythm.

Exercise 1 and 2 - Ascending Only, E String to A string - Half Notes

Exercise 1 is an 8 bar exercise with four bars of the open E string in half notes followed by 4 bars of the open A string in half notes. Here's what the exercise looks like:

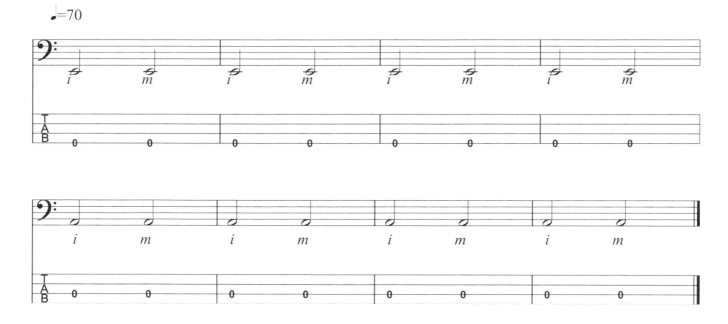

Notes:

(i) As always the tempo is just a guideline. I've got 70 BPM notated at the top of the score...if you have to start at 60 BPM or slower then do so.

(ii) The exercise is *only* 8 bars long. It is important that you don't play the exercise with a longer drum beat.

(iii) If you've been through and mastered prior plucking hand modules the only point where this exercise should be challenging and/or different is going from bar 4 to bar 5, where you move from the open E string to the open A string.

(iv) If need be, practice that movement of the thumb from the open E string to the open A string out of tempo and in isolation from the rest of the exercise. (This is good preparation for this exercise).

When you're comfortable - and the audit point to watch for to know you are feeling comfortable is the transition from the E string to the A string - then reverse which finger you lead with and play this variation of the exercise:

♩=70

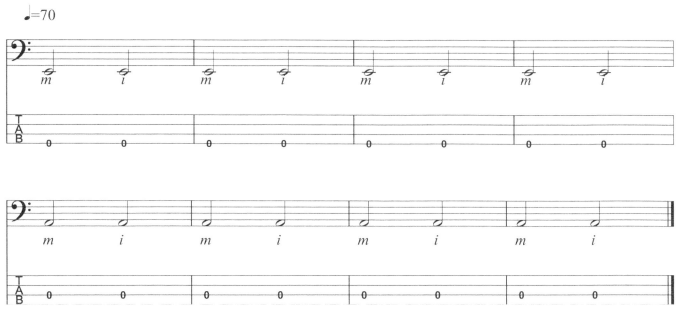

Exercise 3 and 4 - The Rest Stroke - A String To E String

These exercises incorporate the rest stroke and focus on the open A string in half notes over four bars followed by the open E string for 4 bars in half notes:

Module 1.12   49

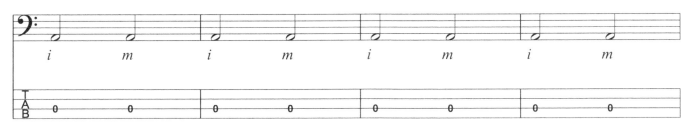

In this exercise the placement of the thumb and its subsequent movement changes. The thumb starts on the top of the E string ready for the fingers to pluck the A string.

In bar 5 the thumb moves to the top of pickup position in order to play the E string.

NOTE THE 'REST STROKE.' The middle finger plays the A string at the end of bar 4 - but the action of the rest stroke with the middle finger coming to rest on the E string means that it's in prime position to play the E string. So that's the finger we use to play the E string at the point of transition.

And the remaining bars continue the guideline of strict alternation of the fingers when playing on the same string or ascending.

PLEASE RE-READ THAT AGAIN CAREFULLY AND CHECK OUT THE VIDEOS ON THE UNIT PAGE SO YOU FOLLOW THIS!

If you start the exercise leading with the middle finger on the A, then the index finger will be the finger that plays the rest stroke at the end of bar 4, and is used for the first plucking hand stroke in bar 5. Like this:

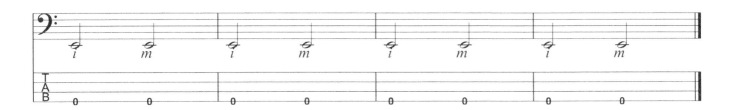

Making This A 16 Bar Exercise:

If we take both of the above examples and extend them to 16 bars by repeating the 8 bars, we get an interesting combination of both of the above exercises. For space reasons, these can be found on the Online Module 1.12 page.

Action Steps

1. Select a practice track tempo that you are comfortable with from the half note practice tracks in your practice library.

2. Start with Exercises 1 and 2 - which are about working on transitioning the thumb from the top of the pick up to the top of the E string as you play the open E string and open A string respectively.

3. Play that several times. Work on the movement of the thumb separately and out of tempo if you need to.

4. To avoid favouring one finger over another make sure that you switch and practice leading with the middle finger.

5. When you are comfortable with this, then move on to Exercises 3 and 4

where you start on the A string and play to the E string. Pay careful attention to the interruption to the strict alternation caused by raking and then continue the strict alternation.

6. When you have played these exercises several times then switch to a 16 bar track and play the final two exercises (Found on the online version of Module 1.12). Focus on plucking with the correct finger when moving from the A string to E string.

Module 1.13 Plucking Hand 7

The next set of exercises will focus on using the two finger rest stroke with the open A string and the open D string.

Exercise 1 and 2 - Ascending Only, A String to D string - Whole Notes

Exercise 1 for this unit is an 8 bar exercise using the open A string and open D string with whole notes. Here's what the exercise looks like:

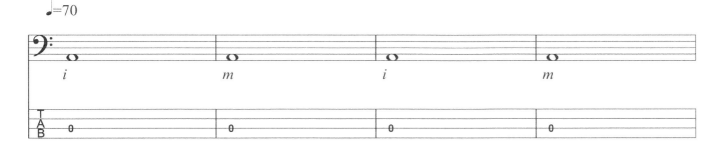

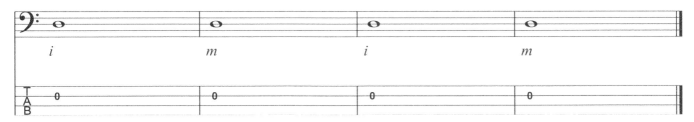

Notes:

(i) As always the tempo is just a guideline. I've got 70 BPM notated at the top of the score...if you have to start at 60 BPM or slower then do so.

(ii) The exercise is ONLY 8 bars long. It is important that you don't play the exercise with a longer drum beat.

(iii) If you've been through and mastered prior modules the ONLY point where this exercise should be challenging and/or different is going from bar 4 to bar 5 where you move from the open A string to the open D string.

(iv) If need be, practice that movement of the thumb from the top of the E string (when playing the A string) to the A string (when playing the D string) out of tempo and in isolation from the rest of the exercise.

When you're comfortable – and the audit point to watch for to know you are feeling comfortable is the transition of the thumb from the E string to the A string – then reverse which finger you lead with and play this variation of the exercise:

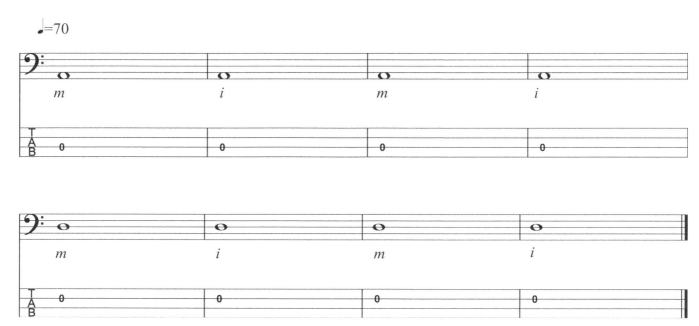

Exercise 3 and 4 - The Rest Stroke - D String To A String

In these exercises the open D string is played before the open A string, which brings the rest stroke into play. Here's the exercise leading with the index finger:

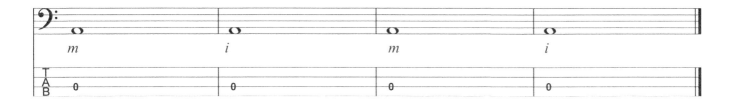

In this exercise the placement of the thumb and its subsequent movement changes. The thumb starts resting on the A string ready for the fingers to pluck the D string.

In bar 5 the thumb moves to the top of the E string in order to play the A string.

BUT NOTE THE 'REST STROKE.' The middle finger plays the last open D string at the end of bar 4 - but the action of the rest stroke with the middle finger coming to rest on the A string means that it's in prime position to play the A string. So that's the finger we use to play the A string at the point of transition.

And the remaining bars continue the guideline of strict alternation of the fingers when playing on the same string or ascending.

PLEASE RE-READ THAT AGAIN CAREFULLY AND CHECK OUT THE VIDEOS ON THE UNIT PAGE SO YOU FOLLOW THIS!

If the alternation is reversed and the middle finger is used to lead, then it will be the index finger that 'rests' on the A string at the end of bar 4 and is used to pluck the first note of bar 5. Like this:

Module 1.13 55

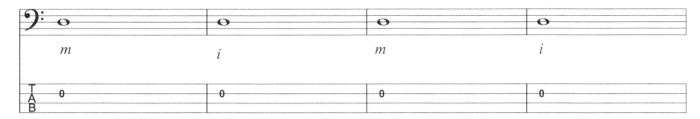

Making This A 16 Bar Exercise:

If we take both of the above examples and extend them to 16 bars by repeating the 8 bars, we get an interesting combination of both of the above exercises. For space reasons, these can be found on the Online Module 1.13 page.

Action Steps

1. Select a practice track tempo that you are comfortable with from the whole note practice tracks in your practice library.

2. Start with Exercises 1 and 2 - which are about working on transitioning the thumb from the E string to the A string as you play the open A string and open D string respectively.

3. Play that several times. Work on the movement of the thumb separately and out of tempo if you need to.

4. To avoid favouring one finger over another make sure that you switch and practice leading with the middle finger.

5. When you are comfortable with this, then move on to Exercises 3 and 4 where you start on the D string and play to the A string. Pay careful

attention to the interruption to the strict alternation caused by raking and then continue the strict alternation.

6. When you have played these exercises several times then switch to a 16 bar track and play the final two exercises (Found on the online version of Module 1.13). Focus on plucking with the correct finger when moving from the D string to the A string.

Module 1.14 - Plucking Hand 8

In this unit, the sequence used in Module 1.13 will be followed to work on plucking hand facility moving from playing the open A string to the open D string, and vice-versa. The rhythmic unit being used for the exercises is half notes.

Exercise 1 and 2 - Ascending Only, A String to D string - Half Notes

Exercise 1 is an 8 bar exercise playing 4 bars of open A strings in half notes, followed by 4 bars of open D strings in half notes:

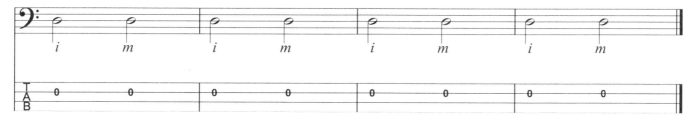

Notes:

(i) As always the tempo is just a guideline. I've got 70 BPM notated at the top of the score...if you have to start at 60 BPM or slower then do so.

(ii) The exercise is *only* 8 bars long. It is important that you don't play the exercise with a longer drum beat.

(iii) If need be, practice the movement of the thumb from the open E string to the open A string out of tempo and in isolation from the rest of the exercise.

When you're comfortable – and the audit point to watch for to know you are feeling comfortable is the transition of the thumb from the E string to the A string – then reverse which finger you lead with and play this variation of the exercise:

Exercise 3 and 4 - The Rest Stroke - D String To A String

The next exercises reverse the direction of plucking and consist of 4 bars of open D string in half notes and then four bars of open A strings in half notes:

In this exercise the placement of the thumb and its subsequent movement changes. The thumb starts on the top of the A string ready for the fingers to pluck the D string.

In bar 5 the thumb moves to the top of the E string in order to play the A string.

NOTE THE 'REST STROKE.' The middle finger plays the D string at the end of bar 4 - but the action of the rest stroke with the middle finger coming to rest on the A string means that it's in prime position to play the A string. So that's the finger we use to play the A string at the point of transition.

And the remaining bars continue the guideline of strict alternation of the fingers when playing on the same string or ascending.

PLEASE RE-READ THAT AGAIN CAREFULLY AND CHECK OUT THE VIDEOS ON THE UNIT PAGE SO YOU FOLLOW THIS!

If this exercise is repeated, but the plucking hand leads with the middle finger on the D string, when we move to the A string it will be the index finger that 'rests' and is used to pluck the first note in bar 5. Like this:

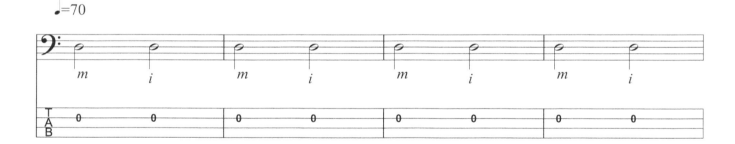

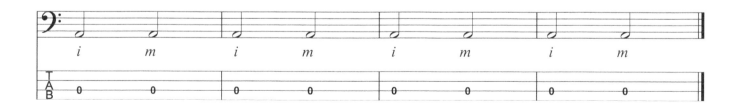

60   Module 1.14

Making This A 16 Bar Exercise:

If we take both of the above examples and extend them to 16 bars by repeating the 8 bars, we get an interesting combination of both of the above exercises. For space reasons, these can be found on the Online Module 1.14 page.

Action Steps

1. Select a practice track tempo that you are comfortable with from the half note practice tracks in your practice library.

2. Start with Exercises 1 and 2 - which are about working on transitioning the thumb from the top of the E string to the top of the A string as you play the open A string and open D string respectively.

3. Play that several times. Work on the movement of the thumb separately and out of tempo if you need to.

4. To avoid favouring one finger over another make sure that you switch and practice leading with the middle finger.

5. When you are comfortable with this, then move on to Exercises 3 and 4 where you start on the D string and play to the A string. Pay careful attention to the interruption to the strict alternation caused by raking and then continue the strict alternation.

6. When you have played these exercises several times then switch to a 16 bar track and play the final two exercises (Found on the online version of Module 1.14). Focus on plucking with the correct finger when moving from the D string to A string.

Module 1.15 Song 2 - "Have I Told You Recently"

"Have I Told You Recently" is a simple, Van Morrison style ballad that has a Verse 1-Verse 2-Bridge format that's repeated twice. The bass line uses just root notes and half notes as the rhythmic unit.

Here's the first verse:

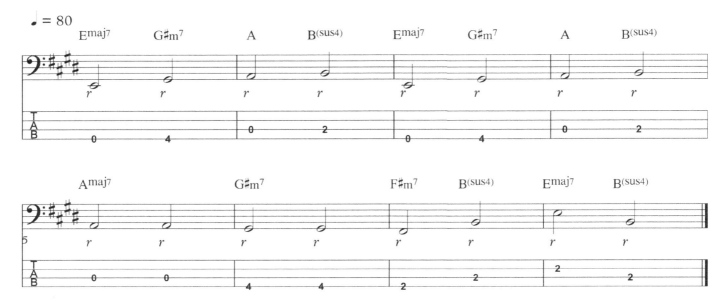

One thing to note when learning song sections in chunks like this: always remember to play to the first note of the next section when you're practicing the song chunks.

Verse 1 is followed by Verse 2. That's almost identical to Verse 1 - so when you're learning Verse 1, remember to finish on an open E string as the first note of the next section.

Here's Verse 2 - and the major difference is that the last chord stays on Emaj7 for the entire bar to set up the first note of the next section, which is an A, being the root note of Amaj7:

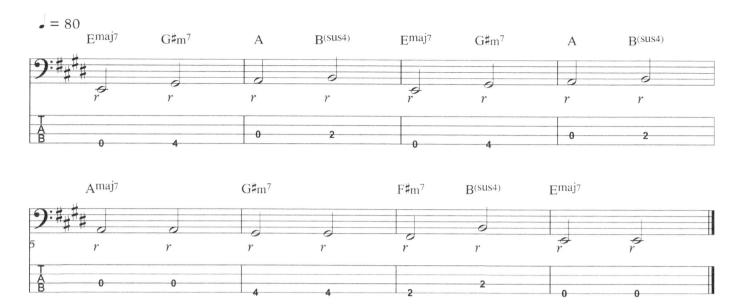

After verse 2, the final section of the song that you need to learn is the bridge. This resolves back to the verse, so finish this section off with a sustained E note. You'll see and hear in the video playalongs of the song chunks on the Module 1.15 page that I end on the first note of the next section too:

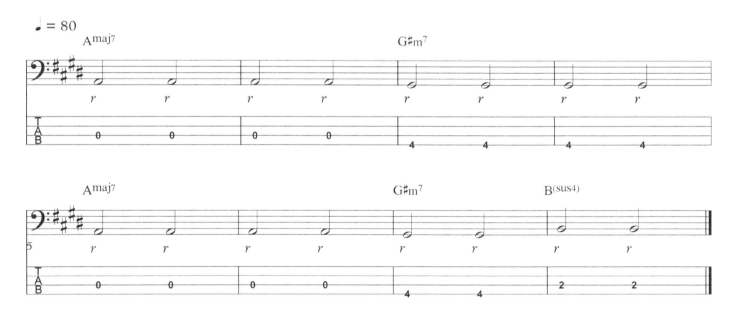

Each of these sections repeats to complete Song #2. Working on this song should help you gain familiarity with some of the sharpened notes on the fretboard.

On the website version of Module 1.15 you'll find a PDF with the song sections arranged together that you can print out and place on your music stand. Additionally there are playalongs of the complete song at different tempo levels, which puts the song sections together like this:

- Verse
- Verse 2
- Bridge
- Verse 3
- Verse 4
- Bridge 2
- Song finishes on an Emaj7 chord, so finish on E.

Module 1.16 Plucking Hand 9

In this unit plucking hand facility will be developed by playing quarter notes on the E and the A string, including the two finger rest stroke. There are two bonus lessons in the online version of the book that are relevant and should be read before starting this Unit. The first bonus lesson deals with counting quarter note rhythms. The second lesson deals with practicing in quarter notes on single strings only. Depending on your facility you may be able to jump straight into this unit.

Exercise 1 and 2 – Ascending Only, E String to A string – Quarter Notes

Exercise 1 is an 8 bar exercise and consists of four bars of open E strings in quarter notes followed by four bars of open A strings in quarter notes. Here's what the exercise looks like:

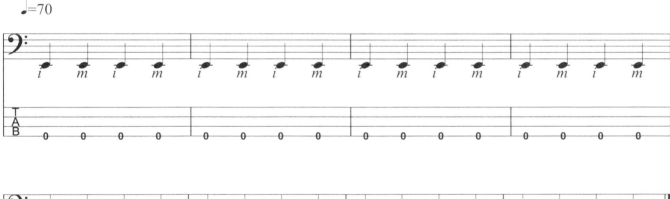

Things to note:

- As always the tempo is just a guideline. I've got 70 BPM notated at the top of the score…if you have to start at 60 BPM or slower then do so. Slow and perfect *always* trumps faster and imperfect.

- The exercise is only 8 bars long.

- If you've been through and mastered prior units the only point where this exercise should be challenging and/or different is going from bar 4 to bar 5 where you move from the open E string to the open A string.

When you're comfortable – and the main audit points are the transition from the E string to the A string along with the quarter note plucking – then reverse which finger you lead with and play this variation of the exercise:

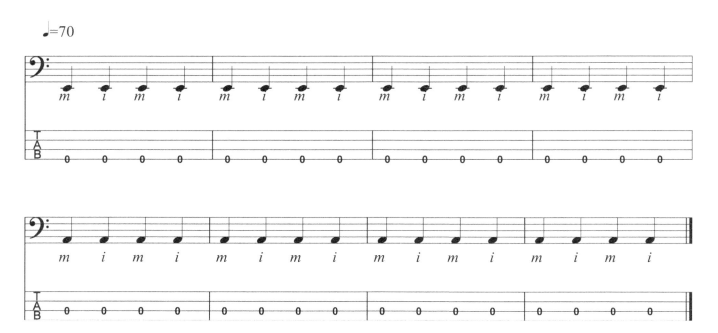

Exercise 3 and 4 – The Rest Stroke – A String To E String

In the next exercises the rest stroke is incorporated by playing the open A string in quarter notes for four bars, and then four bars of open E strings:

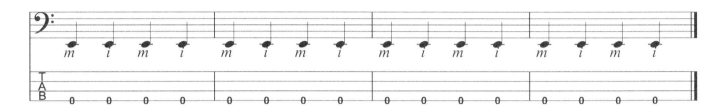

In this exercise the placement of the thumb and its subsequent movement changes. The thumb starts on the top of the E string ready for the fingers to pluck the A string.

In bar 5 the thumb moves to the top of the pick up in order to play the E string.

Note the rest stroke: the middle finger plays the last open A string in bar 4 – but the action of the rest stroke with the middle finger coming to rest on the E string means that it's in prime position to play the E string. So that's the finger used to pluck the E string at the point of transition.

The remaining bars continue the guideline of strict alternation of the index and middle fingers when playing on the same string or ascending.

PLEASE RE-READ THAT AGAIN CAREFULLY AND CHECK OUT THE VIDEOS ON THE UNIT PAGE SO YOU FOLLOW THIS!

If the exercise starts on the A string leading with the middle finger, it will be the index finger that 'rests' and is used in bar 5 when the exercise moves to the E string. Like this:

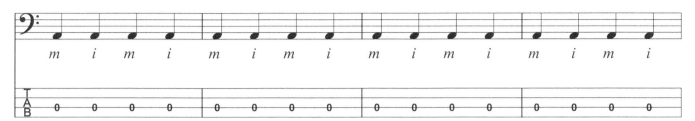

Making This A 16 Bar Exercise:

If we take both of the above examples and extend them to 16 bars by repeating the 8 bars, we get an interesting combination of both of the above exercises. For space reasons, these can be found on the Online Module 1.16 page.

Action Steps

1. Select a practice track tempo that you are comfortable with from the Quarter Note practice tracks in your practice library. (These tracks are available on the online Module 1.16 page).

2. Start with Exercise 1, which focuses on transitioning the thumb from the top of the pick up to the top of the E string as you play the open E string and open A string respectively with the quarter note rhythm.

3. Play that several times. Work on the movement of the thumb separately and out of tempo if you need to.

4. To avoid favouring one finger over another make sure that you switch and practice leading with the middle finger.

5. When you are comfortable with this, then move on to the next two exercises where you start on the A string and reverse the movement and

move downwards. Pay careful attention to the interruption to the strict alternation caused by raking and the rest stroke and then continue the strict alternation.

6. When you have played these exercises several times then switch to a 16 bar long track and play the final two exercises (Found on the online version of Module 1.16). Pay attention to plucking with the correct finger when moving from the A string to E string using the rest stroke.

7. All of the exercises are filmed on the Unit 1.16 page. So please make sure you cross reference the examples with the videos of each exercise.

Module 1.17 Song 3 - "Hey John"

"Hey John" is a simple rock ballad style line based on a Jimi Hendrix style chord progression. This practice song has a Verse 1-Verse 2-Solo format that's repeated twice. The bass line uses just root notes but uses both half notes and quarter notes in the rhythm of the bass line.

Here's the first verse:

You'll note that in bars 3,4,5, and 6 that the annotation '8' is used. This is a root note, but the '8' represents the root note played an octave higher. (There are 8 notes in the major scale...so 8 is used for octave).

Verse 1 is followed by Verse 2. That's almost identical to Verse 1 except that there's a rhythmic change from half notes to quarter notes in bar 8 to set up the change of rhythm for the guitar solo:

The solo is the next section:

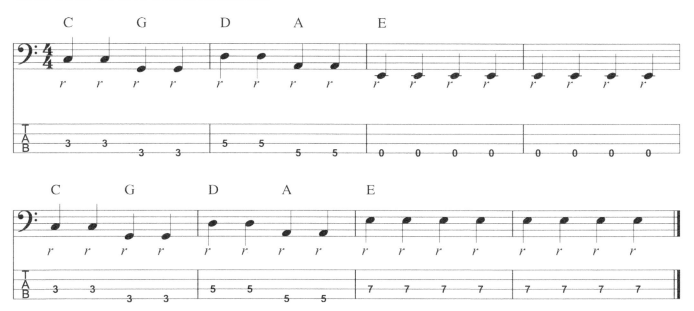

Note that this entire practice piece is played on just the E and A strings, so watch your rest stroke when playing a note on the A string and then playing a note on the E string.

On the website version of Module 1.17 you'll find a PDF with the song sections arranged together that you can print out and place on your music stand. Additionally there are playalongs of the complete song at different tempo levels, which puts the song sections together like this:

- Verse
- Verse 2
- Solo
- Verse 3
- Verse 4
- Solo
- Song finishes on a C chord, so finish on C.

Sidebar: *at the moment the practice songs have simple bass lines. As we introduce more rhythms and more devices over the course of the remaining four modules of this course, that gives the opportunity to revisit these simple practice songs and make the bass lines more interesting.*

Module 1.18 Plucking Hand 10

In this unit plucking hand facility will be developed by playing quarter notes on the A and the D string, including the two finger rest stroke. As well as developing plucking hand facility, focus will also be on the movement of the thumb from the top of the E string (when playing the A string) to the top of the A string (when playing the D string).

Exercise 1 Ascending Only, A String to D string – Quarter Notes

In Exercise 1 we are going to play an 8 bar exercise and we are going to play four bars of open A strings and then four bars of open D strings. Here's what the exercise looks like:

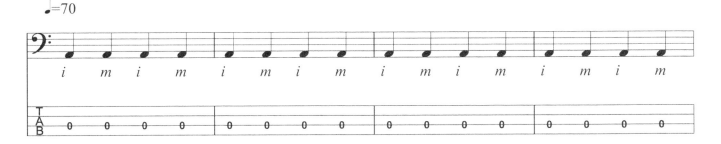

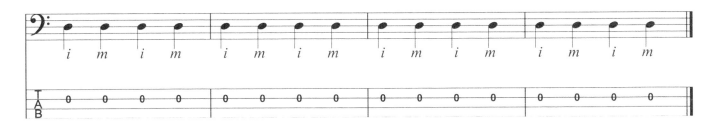

Things to note:

- As always the tempo is just a guideline. I've got 70 BPM notated at the top of the score…if you have to start at 60 BPM or slower then do so. Slow and perfect *always* trumps faster and imperfect.

- The exercise is only 8 bars long.

- If you've been through and mastered prior units the only point where this exercise should be challenging and/or different is going from bar 4 to bar 5 where you move from the open A string to the open D string.

When you're comfortable - and the main point to be watching for to start feeling comfortable is the transition of the thumb from the top of the E string to the top of the A string - then reverse which finger you lead with and play this variation of the exercise:

Exercise 3 and 4 – The Rest Stroke – D String To A String

In the next exercises the rest stroke is incorporated by playing the open D string in quarter notes for four bars, and then four bars of open A strings:

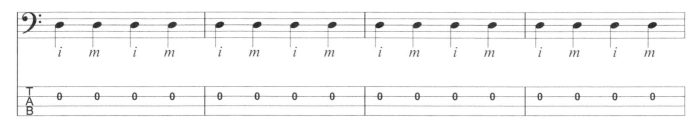

In this exercise the placement of the thumb and its subsequent movement changes. The thumb starts on the top of the A string ready for the fingers to pluck the D string.

In bar 5 the thumb moves to the top of the E string in order to play the A string.

Note the rest stroke: the middle finger plays the last open D string at the end of bar 4 – but the action of the rest stroke with the middle finger coming to rest on the A string means that this finger in prime position to play the A string. So that's the finger we use to pluck the A string at the point of transition.

And the remaining bars continue the guideline of strict alternation of the fingers when playing on the same string or ascending.

PLEASE RE-READ THAT AGAIN CAREFULLY AND CHECK OUT THE VIDEOS ON THE UNIT PAGE SO YOU FOLLOW THIS!

If the exercise starts on the D string leading with the middle finger, it will be the index finger that 'rests' and is used in bar 5 when the exercise moves to the A string. Like this:

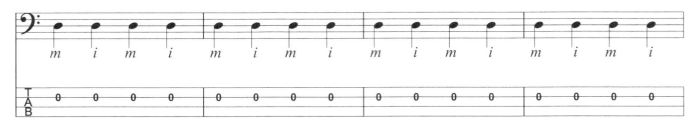

Making This A 16 Bar Exercise:

If we take both of the above examples and extend them to 16 bars by repeating the 8 bars, we get an interesting combination of both of the above exercises. For space reasons, these can be found on the online Module 1.18 page.

Action Steps

1. Select a practice track tempo that you are comfortable with from the Quarter Note practice tracks in your practice library.

2. Start with Exercise 1 which is about working on transitioning the thumb from the top of the E string to the top of the A string as you play the open A string and open D string respectively.

3. Play that several times. Work on the movement of the thumb separately and out of tempo if you need to.

4. To avoid favouring one finger over another make sure that you switch and practice leading with the middle finger.

5. When you are comfortable with this, then move on to the next two exercises where you start on the D string and reverse the movement and move downward to the A string. Pay careful attention to the interruption

to the strict alternation caused by raking and the rest stroke and then continue the strict alternation.

6. When you have played these exercises several times then switch to a 16 bar long track and play the final two exercises (Found on the online version of Module 1.18). Pay attention to plucking with the correct finger when moving from the D string to A string using the rest stroke.

7. All of the exercises are filmed on the Module 1.18 page. So please make sure you cross reference the examples with the videos of each exercise.

Module 1.19 Song 4 - "Every Country Breath You Take"

"Every Country Breath You Take" is a quarter note, country ballad style line based on a Sting chord progression. This practice song has a Verse 1-Verse 2-Bridge format that's repeated twice. The bass line uses just root notes with a quarter note rhythm.

Some notes:

- The tempo has gone up to 100 BPM. I've included practice tracks at slower tempos in the downloads on the Module 1.19 web page. So you can consider 100 BPM as a target tempo and work towards that.

- Although the first 80-20 Bass device introduced so far is the root note, and although this is a common device in the vocabulary of rock and pop, repeated use of the root note can get repetitive and a little predictable quickly. One of the things that will happen throughout the 5 Module programme is that every time a new device and/or a new rhythm is introduced, bonus bass line studies with the song progressions already featured will be added. So you can see how bass lines can be developed.

Here's the first verse:

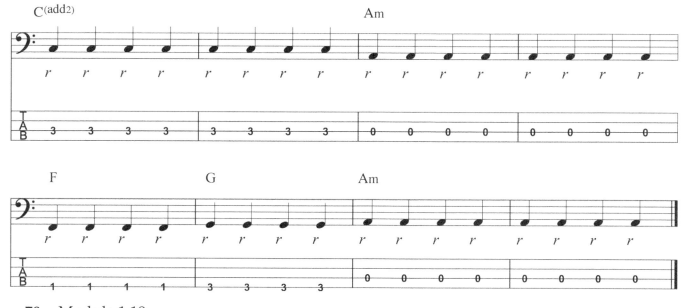

Verse 1 is followed by verse 2. Verse 2 is almost identical, except the last two bars of verse 2 are different from verse 1:

The bridge is the final section to learn:

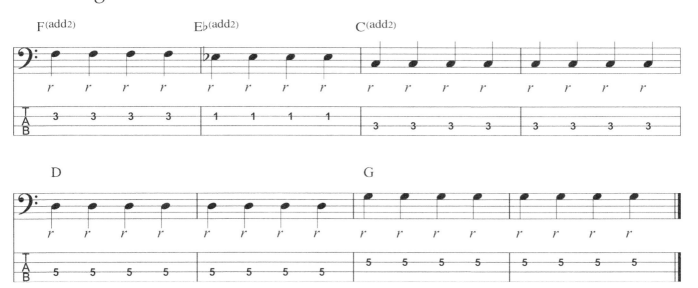

Note that this practice piece is played on the E, A and D strings....so watch your rest stroke when moving between strings.

On the website version of Module 1.19 you'll find a PDF with the song sections arranged together that you can print out and place on your music stand. Additionally there are playalongs of the complete song at different tempo levels, which puts the song sections together like this:

- Verse1
- Verse 2
- Bridge
- Verse 3
- Verse 4
- Bridge 2
- Song finishes on a C(add2) chord, so finish on C.

Module 1.20 Plucking Hand 11

In this unit plucking hand facility will be further developed using quarter notes on all four strings. The exercises in this unit will be repeated throughout the five modules of the course with the most common quarter note and half note rhythms that will be studied in future modules.

Exercise 1 Ascending Only, E String to G string – Quarter Notes

Exercise 1 is a 16 bar exercise and consists of four bars played on each string in turn with a constant, quarter note rhythm. Here's what the exercise looks like:

♩=70

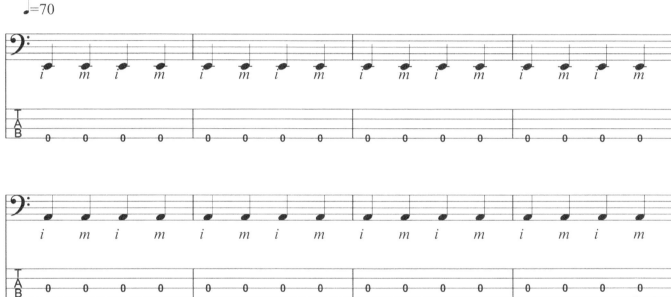

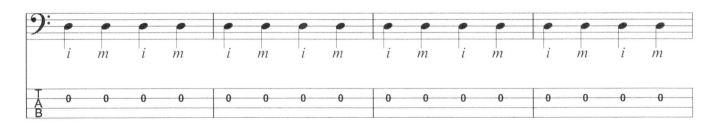

Focus on these elements in this exercise:

- Strict alternation of the fingers.

- A 'smooth and seamless' movement of the thumb when you change strings.

- Precise placement of each note in time with the quarter note pulse.

When you're comfortable with that exercise, then lead with the middle finger:

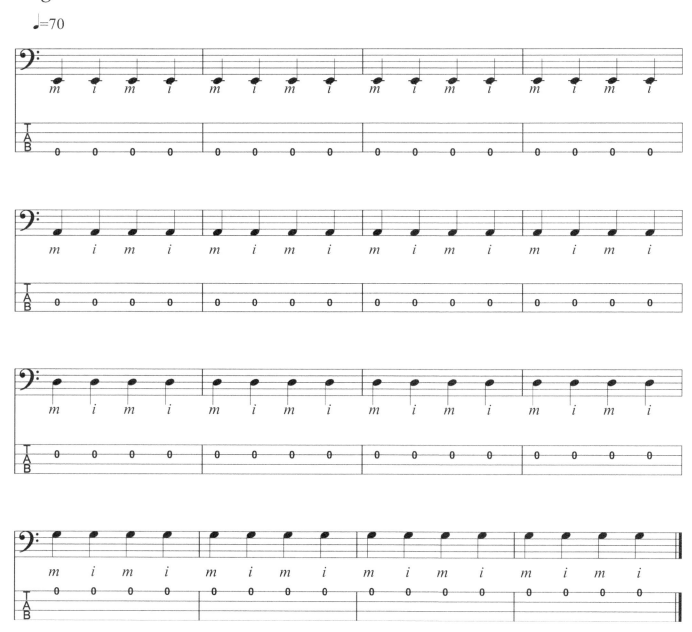

Exercise 3 and 4 – Descending Only, G String to E string – Quarter Notes

Exercise 3 and 4 are also 16 bar exercises. They are the reverse of the previous exercise and descend from G to E. Here's what exercise 3 looks like:

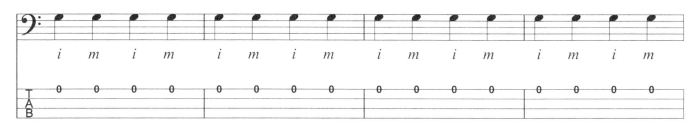

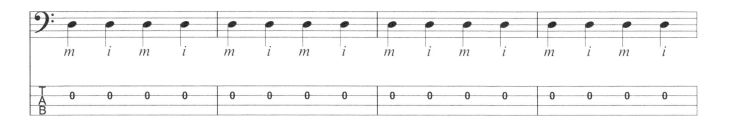

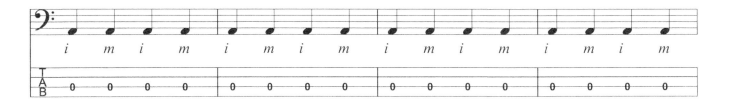

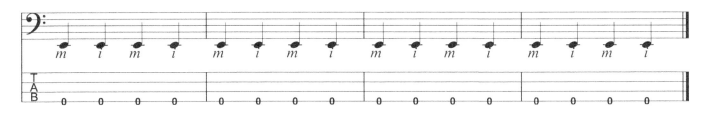

For these exercises, focus on these elements:

- Strict alternation of the fingers.

- A 'smooth and seamless' movement of the thumb when you change strings.

- Leading with the 'raked' finger when changing string.

- Switch alternation once you have 'raked' downwards.

- Precise placement of each note in time with the quarter note pulse.

And here's Exercise 4 which is identical except you lead with the middle finger on the G string:

84   Module 1.20

Action Steps

1. Select a practice track tempo that you are comfortable with from the Quarter Note practice tracks that you downloaded from the Module 1.18 page.

2. Start with Exercise 1 which is about playing from the E string to the G string.

3. Play that several times. Work on the movement of the thumb separately and out of tempo if you need to.

4. To avoid favouring one finger over another make sure that you switch and practice Exercise 2 leading with the middle finger. **Tip:** *you should practice exercises 1 and 2 - and also exercises 3 and 4 - in pairs so that you don't build up a preference for leading with one finger over another.*

5. When you are comfortable with this, then move on to the next two exercises where you start on the G string and reverse the direction and move downwards. Pay careful attention to the interruption to the strict alternation caused by raking and then continue the strict alternation.

6. All of the exercises are filmed on the Unit 1.20 page. So please make sure you cross reference the examples with the videos of each exercise.

Module 1.21 Device 2 - The Root And Fifth

The second 80-20 bass device that we're going to look at is the root and fifth. There is a bonus theory lesson in the online version of the book that gives you some more detail on the note that's called the fifth and why it's called the fifth. Summarizing that lesson, music theory is based on the major scale and the 'fifth' is called that because it's the fifth note in the major scale. In the key of C, the fifth is G. In the key of F, the fifth is C.

Here's a practice progression that goes from C7 to F7 using quarter notes where the bass line is made up of roots and fifths - and the fifths are annotated with '5' underneath them:

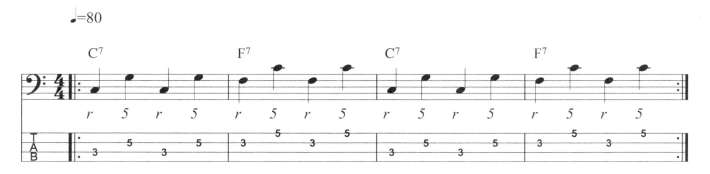

The fifth can also be played below the root note, where it's known as the 'lower 5th.' Here's the same example but this time with lower 5ths in the C7 bars - note that this time the annotation for the root note has changed to '8.' That's to signify that you're playing the root note above the fifth - where it could be thought of as the octave. Also note that the roots and 5ths for the F7 bars are played an octave lower:

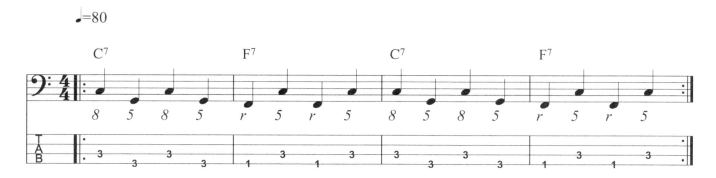

In Module 1.9 when the root note was introduced, an exercise using the root note with half notes and the common chord progression of C to Am to F to G7 was used.

Here's the same chord progression but this time the rhythm is quarter notes, and the practice exercise is created using roots and fifths:

Note that if the root is annotated with an '8,' that means that you're playing down to the lower 5th.

If you compare this practice example with the example in Module 1.9, you'll hear that the addition of the 5th into the bass line gives this line much more movement.

As more devices are added to the vocabulary of ideas that can be used in realistic sounding lines, the previous songs can be adapted and made more interesting. This is something that will pay off when several more devices have been introduced.

To give you an idea though, here's Verse 1 of "Every Country Breath You Take" reworked to use root and fifth, instead of just the root note:

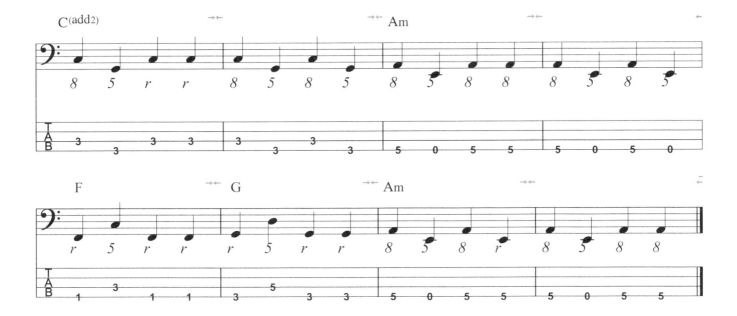

If you compare this with the previous example, you should see the similarity in terms of the chord progression between this verse and the common chord progression of C to Am to F to G7.

In Module 1.9 there was a practice example that featured root notes and half notes being used to play through the 12 bar blues.

In the next practice example, the blues is played through with a quarter note rhythm, and fifths are added as well as root notes. Remember that where a note is annotated as an '8,' that means it's a root note that's played *above* the fifth that follows:

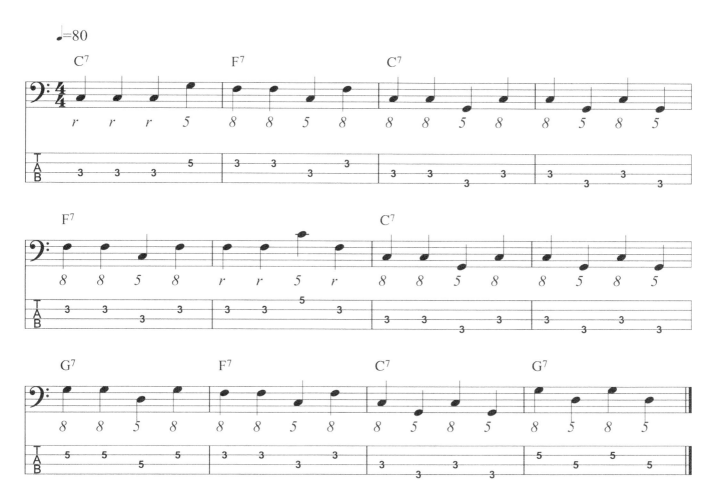

The root and fifth is one of the most common devices found in bass lines, it's a sound that you'll recognize when we play through the rest of the practice song progressions in this first Module. As well as being a device on it's own, the root (or octave) and fifth are notes that you'll find in Devices 4, 5, 6, 8, 9 and 10. All these devices will be studied in future modules in this series. Learning and practicing roots and fifths thoroughly is foundational "Bass IQ" knowledge which you'll build upon as you learn more.

Module 1.22 Fretboard Mastery 1

Knowing the locations and note names of all the notes on the fretboard is a basic discipline – yet one that few beginners do in an organized and disciplined fashion.

The benefits of taking some time now to learn the notes of the fretboard are that once learned and memorized, you never have to do this again. And this is foundational knowledge that you need to have under your belt in order to proceed.

There are only 12 notes in western music. The series of exercises systematically work through each note, starting from the lowest pitch note on a conventionally tuned 4 string bass, the open E string.

How this exercise works is that you select one note at a time to work on, and you start from low to high (or high to low) and play that note in every location that it appears on your bass.

In this Unit, the note locations to learn are for the note E. This exercise should be done out of tempo. In the video that accompanies this - available on the online version of Module 1.22 - I refer several times to the fact that these fretboard mastery exercises work perfectly as warm up exercises. So it is easy to incorporate these exercises into your practice plan.

Please cross reference the video, but what you should be aiming for is to be able to play this first exercise – which is for a 4 String Bass with 21 frets, and includes all the possible locations of E:

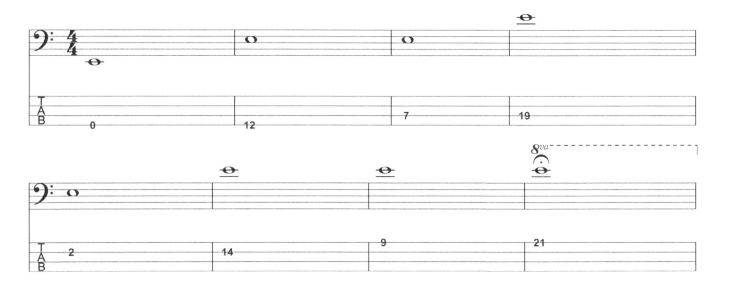

Each time you play a note, you should say 'E' to yourself. This reinforces the name of the note and where it can be found on the fretboard.

Note that the way this exercise is structured is that you play all the 'E' notes on the lowest string first – that's the E string of course. And then you play all the 'E' notes on the A string. And then all the 'E' notes on the D string. And finally all the 'E' notes on the G string.

Over time the practicing of this exercise – and the similar exercises for all the other notes – will improve your facility and confidence when playing on the bass.

Once you can play this exercise in an 'ascending' fashion, then learn it in a descending fashion too – so start at the highest 'E' note on the G string and then play the next 'E' note on the G string. And then move to the D string….and so on.

Here's how it looks in notation and tab:

Module 1.22

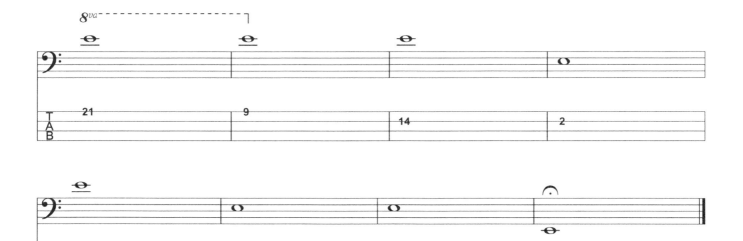

I've also prepared a 'fretboard chart' that you can print out if required to use as a cross-reference to assist remembering the different locations on the bass for the note 'E.' That is on the online Module 1.22 page.

Module 1.23 Plucking Hand 12

In this unit the exercises from Module 1.20 are repeated. The crucial difference is that the focus switches to increasing the tempo. The goal tempo of these exercises is 100 BPM.

Exercise 1 Ascending Only, E String to G string – Quarter Notes

Exercise 1 consists of four bars on each open string, but the exercise goal tempo is 100 BPM:

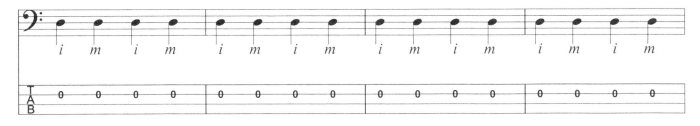

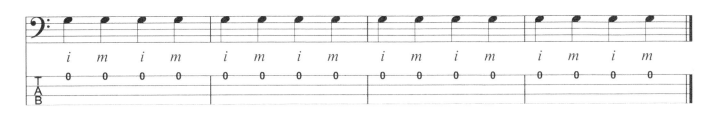

Focus on these elements in this exercise:

- Strict alternation of the fingers.

- A 'smooth and seamless' movement of the thumb when you change strings.

- Precise placement of each note in time with the quarter note pulse.

When you're comfortable with that exercise, then lead with the middle finger:

♩=100

Exercise 3 and 4 – Descending Only, G String to E string – Quarter Notes

Exercise 3 and 4 are also 16 bar exercises. They are the reverse of the previous exercise and descend from G to E. Here's what exercise 3 looks like:

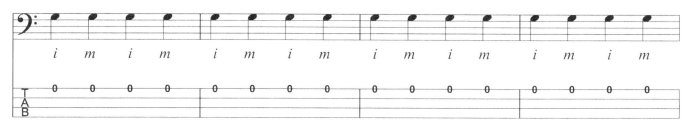

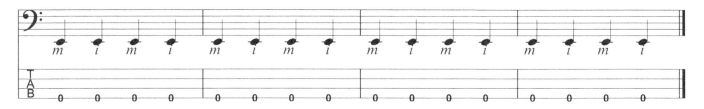

For these exercises, focus on these elements:

- Strict alternation of the fingers.
- A 'smooth and seamless' movement of the thumb when you change strings.

- Leading with the 'raked' finger when changing string.
- Switch alternation once you have 'raked' downwards.
- Precise placement of each note in time with the quarter note pulse.

And here's Exercise 4 which is identical except you lead with the middle finger on the G string:

Action Steps

1. On the Module 1.23 page are quarter note practice tracks that range in tempo from 75 BPM to 100 BPM in 5 BPM increments. Depending on your proficiency with the plucking hand, it make take several iterations to work up to 100 BPM and won't be something accomplished in one or two practice sessions.

2. Start with Exercise 1 which is about playing from the E string to the G string.

3. Play that several times. Work on the movement of the thumb separately and out of tempo if you need to.

4. To avoid favouring one finger over another make sure that you switch and practice Exercise 2 leading with the middle finger. **Tip:** *you should practice exercises 1 and 2 - and also exercises 3 and 4 - in pairs so that you don't build up a preference for leading with one finger over another.*

5. When you are comfortable with this, then move on to the next two exercises where you start on the G string and reverse the direction and move downwards. Pay careful attention to the interruption to the strict alternation caused by raking and then continue the strict alternation.

6. All of the exercises are filmed on the Unit 1.23 page. Make sure you cross reference the examples with the videos of each exercise.

Module 1.24 Fretting Hand 3

Digital Permutations

The one finger per fret exercise that we've already done is the most basic digital permutation. But if you think about bass lines you already know you'll realize that rarely will you play a line in a real world song where you fret with the first finger, then the second finger, then the third finger and finally the fourth finger.

So fretting hand technique has to be adaptable to fret notes with different fingers in different orders. That's where digital permutations come in.

There are four sets of digital permutations that will be covered in the upcoming modules. Each set starts with a different finger and covers all the different possible permutations starting with that finger.

So if we start with the first finger, there are only six possible combinations using each of the four fretting hand fingers, and only using each fretting hand fingers once:

- 1 2 3 4
- 1 2 4 3
- 1 3 2 4
- 1 3 4 2
- 1 4 2 3
- 1 4 3 2

The Digital Permutation Exercise (Part 1)

Here's how the exercise for this Unit works – and initially you can start this out of tempo:

(i) You are going to play each successive four finger grouping in turn.

(ii) You are focusing on the following elements of fretting hand technique:

- Fretting with the fingertips.

- Moving ONLY the finger or fingers that needs to move in order to play the next note.

- Keeping fingertips close to the string.

- When playing higher numbered fingers, the lower number fingers stay in contact with the string

Let's just walk through the playing of the 1-2-4-3 Permutation to make sure everything is clear (and cross reference the video too):

- The first note of this permutation is the first finger….so fret the first note with the first finger (say at Fret 5).

- The second note of this permutation is the second finger….so fret the next note with the second finger (which would be at fret 6).

- The third note of this permutation is the fourth finger….so fret the next note with the fourth finger which would be at fret 8. **IMPORTANT:** when the fourth finger goes down, so does the third finger!

- The fourth note of this permutation is the third finger….to fret this at Fret 7, lift off the fourth finger slightly.

Follow this methodology for each permutation – which I'll walk through on the video too – and take it slowly enough that you can exert conscious control of your fingers to prevent excess finger movement.

What About The Double Bass Fingering System And Digital Permutations?

If you wanted to you could also do digital permutations with the double bass fingering system. Obviously only using three fingers there are far less mathematical permutations.

Personally I don't do digital permutations on the double bass system – your fingers are getting enough work on independence and strength by practicing digital permutations on the one finger per fret system.

If you did want to work on double bass system digital permutations, then here are the permutations beginning with the first finger:

- 1 2 4
- 1 4 2

Now most western music is based on rhythmic groupings of four, so you could extend this exercise out by doubling up some notes and having these permutations:

- 1 2 4 2
- 1 2 4 1
- 1 4 2 4
- 1 4 2 1

As noted above, my personal belief is that you don't need to practice double bass system digital permutations provided you are doing your one finger per fret digital permutations.

REMEMBER: *this practice is to be done slowly. You want to be able to exert conscious control on your fingers at all times. In fact this practice should be done so slowly that it can do double duty and work as a warm up exercise.*

My tempo guidelines are these: play each note as a whole note (that leasts for four beats) and set the tempo to 50 or 60 BPM. The online version of the Module 1.24 page has got an overview video that walks through this Unit and reinforces the learnings and the methodology.

Module 1.25 Fretting Hand 4

The digital hand permutation exercises introduced in the previous module, when practiced slowly and correctly, are a great way to build digital independence and control of the fretting hand fingers. But they need to be combined with other exercises fretted in the same manner, in whole notes at 50 or 60 BPM, to extend the control of the fretting hand fingers to more realistic settings.

The exercises for this are adapted from the piano Hanon exercises. These were a series of exercises for piano to develop technique and fluency and speed. Here's the first Hanon adapted for bass so you can see and hear the kind of exercises to adapt:

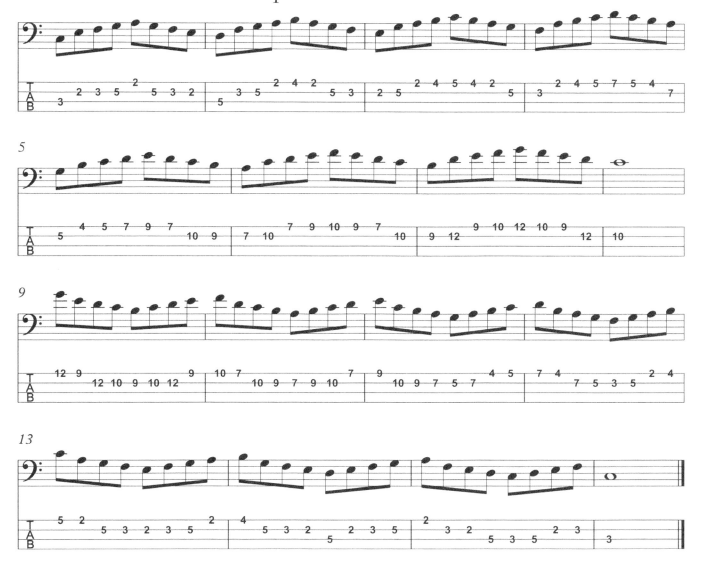

Over time you could build up to playing these kind of exercises at higher tempos in 8th notes. I often adapt them for students to work on 16th note rhythms. Personally I don't use hanons adapted for bass for building technique and speed because the musical ideas being practiced have little relevance to the musical ideas you will use in 95% and more of your bass playing if you're a rock and pop player.

However they are good exercises to use in conjunction with the digital permutation exercises to build control of the fretting hand fingers. The exercise on the previous page can be split into two: an ascending exercise, and a descending exercise.

The ascending exercise is on the following page. Here are the guidelines:

- This exercise is to be played no faster than 60 BPM in whole notes.

- Notes should be fretted with the fingertips of the fingers.

- The fingertips of the fretting hand fingers should be as close to the strings as possible at all time.

- There should be minimal movement of the fretting hand fingers at all times.

- Follow the fretting hand guidelines established in earlier Units. If you are fretting with the 2nd finger, then the 1st finger should be in contact with the string as well. If fretting with the 3rd finger, the 1st and 2nd fingers should be in contact with the string. And if fretting with the 4th finger, all fingers should be in contact with with the string.

Because this exercise, and the descending version of the exercise, are too long to fit onto one page, I've added a PDF version that you can download from the Module 1.25 page so that you can print a copy of the exercises and put it on your music stand in your practice space.

2

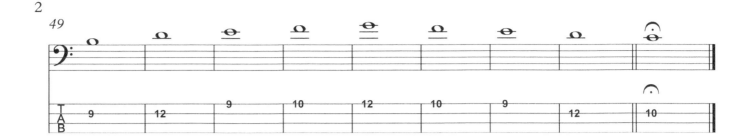

The descending version of Bass Hanon 1 can also be used as a fretting hand exercise in the same fashion as the ascending version. The guidelines for the descending version remain the same:

- This exercise is to be played no faster than 60 BPM in whole notes.

- Notes should be fretted with the fingertips of the fingers.

- The fingertips of the fretting hand fingers should be as close to the strings as possible at all time.

- There should be minimal movement of the fretting hand fingers at all times.

- Follow the fretting hand guidelines established in earlier Units. If you are fretting with the 2nd finger, then the 1st finger should be in contact with the string as well. If fretting with the 3rd finger, the 1st and 2nd fingers should be in contact with the string. And if fretting with the 4th finger, all fingers should be in contact with with the string.

Here's the descending version of the exercise:

2
49

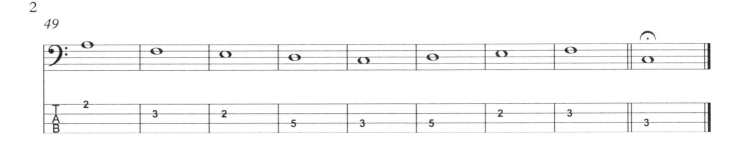

Sidebar: *my advice when you're practicing is to only focus on the fretting hand guidelines for these fretting hand exercises. If you maintain that focus for the exercises, and do them every practice day, that will train the brain that this is how you want the fretting hand to operate. Over time, provided that practice is consistent, those fretting hand guidelines (playing with fingertips, minimal finger movement, fingers close to the strings and so on) will start to appear in your playing.*

Module 1.26 Fretboard Mastery 2

In Module 1.22 we started learning the fretboard by focusing on the note E and playing it in every location on the bass.

In the overview video that went with Module 1.22, I also talked through some 'patterns' that you'll find that occur on the bass guitar fretboard due to the way it is tuned. Specifically:

- The double dot at the 12th fret represents the same notes as occur at the nut (i.e. the open strings) – only an octave above. And the arrangement that occurs from frets 0 to 11 repeats on each string starting at fret 12 marked with the double dot.

- By playing two frets higher and two strings higher you'll also get a repeat of a note but an octave higher.

- By playing one string higher BUT five frets back you'll get another iteration of that note.

So bearing these in mind – and cross reference with the overview video too – if I tell you that the second note we are going to look at is F, and that the lowest occurrence of that note is at the first fret of the E string you can already make some inferences about where other F notes will occur:

- One fret beyond the 12th fret of the E string will be an F – an octave higher than the first note (so played at the 13th fret of the E string).

- Two frets above the 1st fret and two strings above will be F – also an octave higher (so played at the third fret of the D string).

- If the 13th fret of the E string is an F, then if we move up a string and count back 5 frets we'll also get an F. This is the 8th fret of the A string.

- We can get an octave of THAT note by going up two strings and two frets – so from A8 to G10.

And so on.

Try working out the locations yourself if possible.

Once you know how symmetrical the bass fretboard is it makes the job of learning the fretboard much easier. To summarize, here are the locations of F on the various strings:

- E String – 1st fret and 13th fret.
- A String – 8th fret and 20th fret.
- D String – 3rd fret and 15th fret.
- G String – 10th fret and 22nd fret.

Now if you have Precision bass, or a bass modeled on the Precision, you won't be able to hit that note at the 22nd fret because the Precision only has 21 frets!

Here's the ascending exercise finding all the F notes noted out for 21 Fret basses, and note that if your bass has F at the 22nd fret of the G string, then add it into the exercise:

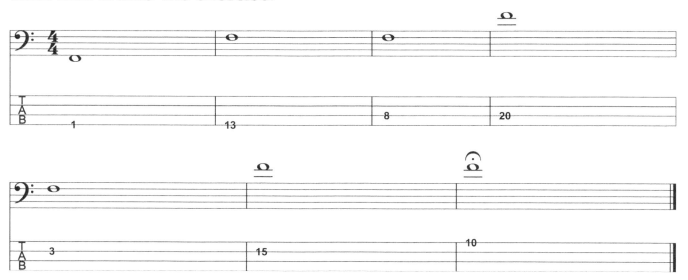

Note that you start at the lowest occurrence of this note on the E string, and then play the next 'F' note on the E string. And then move to the A string and play the lowest 'F' note on the A string….and so on.

When you're comfortable with the locations, then reverse the direction and start with the highest 'F' on the G String. (If you have a 22 fret or greater bass, then insert a high 'F' at the 22nd fret into this exercise):

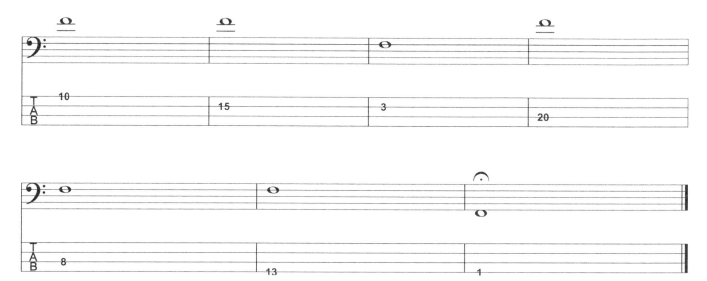

Remember that these exercises are to be played slowly and out of time – and make sure you say 'F' to yourself every time you play one of the F notes to help reinforce the learning.

I've prepared a 'fretboard chart' that you can print out which shows all of the note locations for 'F' on a simulation of a fretboard layout. (Forgive the relatively primitive nature of this – my Photoshop skills are not the best in the world). You'll find that on the online version of Module 1.26.

Module 1.27 More Practice With The 5th

The root and fifth is such a strong combination of notes to use in bass lines that you can create entire bass lines just using this. Country two beat, two beat jazz, and modern reggae all lean heavily on root and fifth. But they're not the only genres of music where you will find use of the root and fifth.

In this unit we're going to introduce the cycle of fifths, and then an exercise which you can use in combination with the cycle of fifths to play root and 5th in all 12 keys. For those of you who are still learning the fingerboard, this exercises is broken down into a sequential learning series that makes learning easier the exercise easier.

The Cycle Of 5ths

The Cycle of 5ths can be represented in diagrammatic form and looks like this:

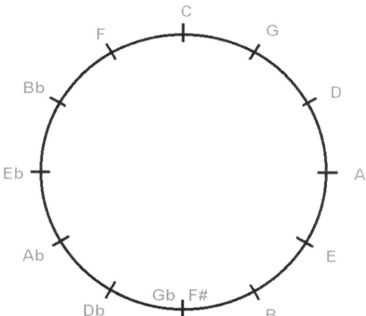

If you look closely, you'll find that all 12 notes on the bass are represented on this cycle. If you go anti-clockwise around the cycle - for example C to

F, F to Bb, Bb to Eb and so on - the musical distance between each pair of notes stays the same. If you go clockwise around the cycle - for example C to G, or G to D or D to A - the musical distance between each pair of notes also stays the same.

The musical distance between notes is more commonly known as an *interval*. If you know where C is on your A string (3rd fret) and know where F and G are on your A string (8th and 10th frets respectively) then you can count the number of frets to get from C to F or C to G. Each one fret movement on the bass is equivalent to the smallest interval in music, which is a semi-tone.

To get from C to F is a movement of 5 frets, or 5 semi-tones. To get from C to G is a movement of 7 frets, or 7 semi-tones.

The Cycle of 5ths is a useful theory tool, but it's also a useful practice tool as well. If you are practicing a musical idea in the key of C for example, you can choose a direction to use and change the key to the next note on the cycle. And then the next. In that way, the cycle becomes a practice guide to practicing something in every key.

The exercise in this Unit is going to do exactly that, and will use root and fifths in every key with half notes.

Root And 5ths In All 12 Keys

To make this exercise simpler to start with for those students just learning the fretboard, this exercise will be broken down into sequential exercises. The first exercise will be root notes only in whole notes. The second exercise will be roots notes and fifths in a half note rhythm. Additionally, with both exercises, each 12 bar exercise will be broken down into three 4 bar chunks.

If you don't need to work through the sub-exercises, then skip to the main 12 bar exercise.

These exercises are going to use the movement of C to F, and F to Bb, that's found by going anti-clockwise around the cycle. The first four notes are C, F, Bb and Eb and the first sub-exercise plays those notes in whole notes:

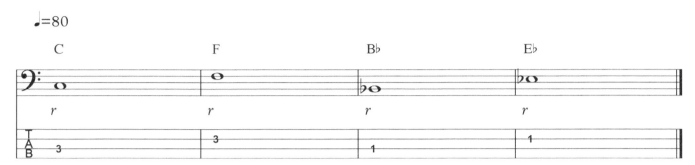

Practice Tip: *whenever a musical exercise is broken down into chunks to make learning easier, always build 'what happens next' into your chunk practice. If you look at the cycle diagram, you'll see that the next note in the cycle is Ab. If you watch the video that goes with this example on the Module 1.27 page, you'll hear that I finish off with a sustained Ab. That way, when you're putting the chunks together, you don't have to learn the transition between the chunks as an additional exercise.*

The next four notes on the cycle after Eb are Ab, Db, F# and B. They are the four root notes for the chords in the next sub-exercise:

Note again that I'm building in the transition to the next chunk at the end of this exercise by playing the first note of the *next* exercise. That note is E and played with the open E string. You'll hear that on the video version of the exercise.

The final set of notes in the cycle are E, A, D and G and they are the root notes for the chords in the next sub-exercise:

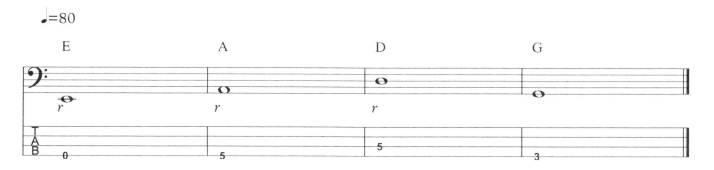

Note that even though this is the last four bars of the exercise, that I play the 'next' note of the cycle at the end of the exercise and go back to C.

With each of these exercises, work through them carefully using the tab locations on the notation/tab examples as a guide as to where to play the notes. Start out slowly and out-of-tempo with each sub-exercise and play the note locations. When you are comfortable with each exercise, they can be combined into a 12 bar exercise:

Although only root notes are being played in this exercise, playing through this kind of cycle exercise will help your facility on the bass as you are forced to play in all 12 key centres.

Once you're comfortable with this exercise, then the chunking down process can be repeated with the goal of being able to play Exercise 1 - which uses the cycle of 5ths, root notes and 5ths, and a half note rhythm. So the first 4 bars chunked down looks like this:

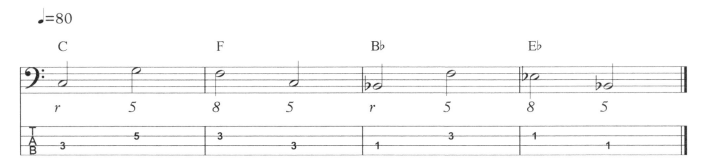

As with the previous exercises, thinking forwards to the next chunk should be built into your process. The first note of the next chunk is Ab - so you'll hear that on the video examples on the Module 1.27 page.

Here's the next 4 bar chunk which starts on Ab:

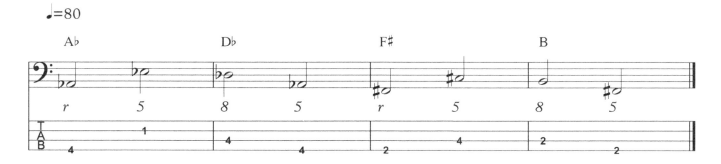

The first note of the next chunk is E. So the previous 4 bar chunk will end with E. Here's the last 4 bar chunk:

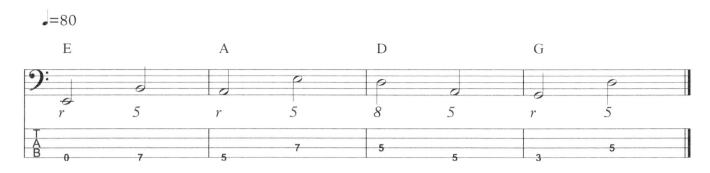

Once you've mastered the individual 4 bar chunks, then they can be combined to create the full 12 bar exercise:

There are practice tracks at different tempo levels for both the individual 4 bar chunks and the complete 12 bar exercise. These can be downloaded from the online version of the Module 1.27 page.

This exercise is a great practice exercise that exposes you to these musical elements:

- Probably the most common device in bass lines - the root and 5th - in all 12 keys.

- As well as the rhythmic elements of the practice track (i.e. the drums), there are harmonic elements too. This gives subliminal ear training in two areas: hearing the quality of the chords (major chords); hearing the movement of C to F or F to Bb. This chord movement is the most commonly used two chord movement in rock and pop.

- A bass line rhythm that you'll find in ballads, as well as sometimes in more up tempo songs.

- One of the primary uses of the root and 5th device is to play from one chord to the next where the root note movement of the two chords is found by going anti-clockwise around the cycle of 5ths.

So although this is a practice exercise, it has direct real world relevance to bass players. In the remaining practice songs, you'll get more exposure to how this can be used in a song context.

Learning Tip: *the more your practice exercises align to how bass lines are played in the real world, the easier you'll find it to learn real world bass lines.*

Module 1.28 Song#5 Bad Moon Falling

Although Song #4 had a bass line in quarter notes, Song #5 goes back to a half note rhythm. The reason for this will become clear as you work through the remaining units in this module. "Bad Moon Falling" has a country rock kind of vibe, and the bass line for this practice song is a kind of line that is sometimes known as a 'country two beat" line.

This practice song uses root notes, roots note and fifths, and uses these with a half note rhythm.

The format of the practice song is Verse-Chorus-Verse-Chorus-Verse-Chorus-Outro Chorus.

Some notes:

- The tempo has gone up to 160 BPM. If you have worked on your quarter note plucking hand tempos...anything over 80BPM for that will ensure that this is no problem. There are also practice tracks at slower tempos that you can use to work up to the 160 BPM target tempo if needed.

- Although the first 80-20 Bass device introduced so far is the root note, and although this is a common device in the vocabulary of rock and pop, repeated use of the root note can get repetitive and a little predictable quickly. One of the things that will happen throughout the 5 Module programme is that every time a new device and/or a new rhythm is introduced, bonus bass line studies with the song progressions already featured will be added. So you can see how bass lines can be developed.

The notation and tab for the first verse is on the following page. You'll see two new musical conventions to tell you about:

- at the start and end of the four bar section are what are known as repeat bars. At the start, is a 'start repeat bar' symbol. That consists of two vertical lines and a colon. At the end of bar 4 is an 'end repeat bar symbol.' That consists of a colon and then two vertical lines. Those symbols instruct you to repeat the bars within the two symbols.

- That repeat instruction is modified by the line of text above bar 4 that says 'Play 4 Times.' Sometimes you'll see that instruction written as 'Play 4X' or even just '4X.'

The combination of the start/end repeat bars, and the 'Play 4 Times' written modification, makes the verse 16 bars long. Here's the notation and tab:

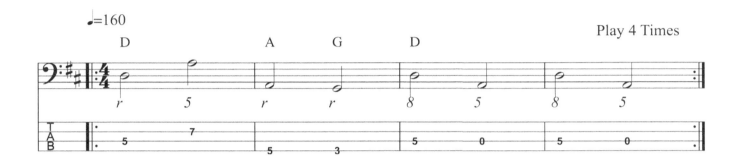

The verse leads directly to the chorus:

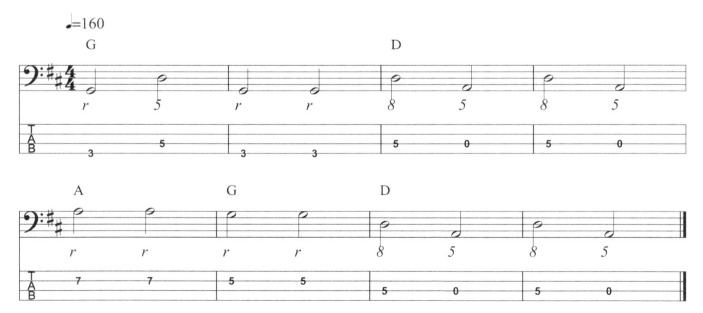

118 Module 1.28

Verse 2, Chorus 2 and Verse 3 are simply repeats of the previous sections.

Chorus 3 has got a minor variation which is to play a quarter note pattern in bar 8:

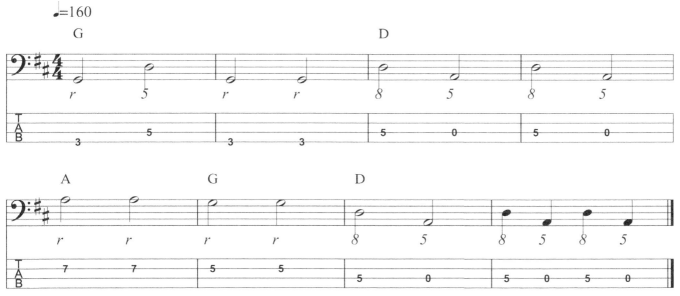

If you find that you can't play that quarter note bar (yet) at this tempo, then just play the bar 8 from Chorus 1.

The outro chorus finishes the song off, and note that the last bar of Chorus 3 (above) is repeated to give a rhythmic push to the sustained chord that finishes the song:

On the website version of Module 1.28 you'll find a PDF with the song sections arranged together that you can print out and place on your music stand for practice and playing purposes.

Additionally there are playalongs of the complete song at different tempo levels, which puts the song sections together like this:

- Verse1
- Chorus 1
- Verse 2
- Chorus 2
- Verse 3
- Chorus 3
- Outro Chorus.

Module 1.29 Quarter Notes With Rests

In this unit looking at playing quarter notes with rests will include rhythm theory, plucking hand exercises AND some fretting hand exercises! It makes more sense to combine these elements into one unit than split the individual parts out into separate and shorter units

Quarter Notes and Rests

So far the quarter note plucking hand exercises covered have used a constant rhythm. While a constant quarter note rhythm does happen in real world bassline, it's just as common - if not more so - to find quarter note bass lines that include rests.

Definition: *A Rest can be thought of a rhythmic subdivision – e.g. a whole note, a half note, a quarter note, an eighth note or a sixteenth note – where nothing sounds.*

Here's the basic rhythm that we're going to be looking at in this Unit played on the open E string:

In some ways this is superficially similar to the half note exercise – the notes are played on Beats 1 and 3 as you'll see if you'll check this version with the subdivisions of the bar enumerated out:

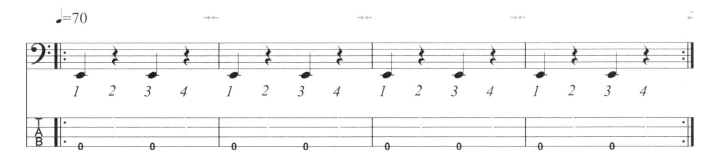

And compare and contrast that with the half note example from earlier in this Module:

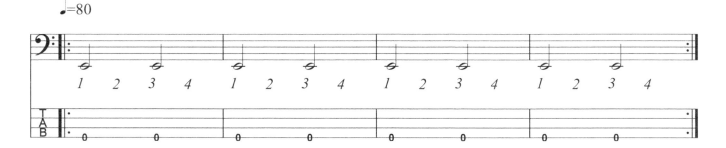

In both of these examples the notes are played on Beats 1 and 3 of each bar – the primary difference is the duration of the note. In the latter example the notes last for two beats and there's no gap between them but in the first example the notes only last for a beat and there is a defined period that lasts for a beat where nothing is happening in the bass line.

To illustrate this so you can clearly hear the sound of these two examples – and more importantly the difference in the sound between the quarter note with rests example and the half notes example – I've filmed a composite example with 8 bars of quarter notes on beats 1 and 3 with rests, and then 8 bars of half notes. Listen carefully to the composite example to hear the distinct difference.

Now the focus switches to how to play the quarter note with rest rhythm and to do that, the topic of 'muting' needs to be introduced.

Playing The Rest

A 'rest' by its definition is defined as an absence of something, and often in bass literature you'll hear talk about 'leaving space' or similar. When it comes to actually incorporating rests into your playing I like to be more proactive and think of the rest as an integral part of a bar's rhythm (which it is) and then think of 'playing the rest.'

Now to actively play the rest we need to talk about muting. Up to now we've talked about muting predominantly in connection with the plucking hand rest stroke and we've talked a little about it in connection with using the fretting hand to stop the sound of unwanted higher open strings sounding when doing some of our rest stroke exercises.

There are three ways of actively muting a note, two of these involve the fretting hand and one involves the plucking hand. The plucking hand muting – which I'll cover so that you are aware of it - is an advanced topic that we won't be working on in the HTPB#50 Course.

Here are the different way of muting strings, one by one.

Muting System 1 – The Fretting Hand/Open Strings

In the first exercise I've superimposed a downwards arrow on Beats 2 and 4:

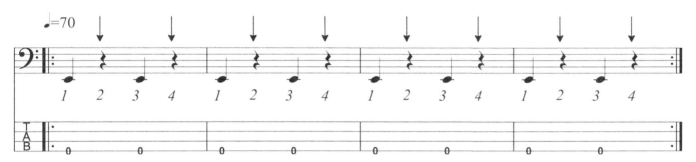

That downwards arrow represents the motion that you have to make with your fretting hand to mute the open E string on Beat 2. If you watch the video on the online version of the Module 1.29 page you'll see how I do it.

Things to note:

- Ideally you want to mute with more than one finger – this helps avoid pressing down on what are called harmonic nodes and getting a harmonic to chime when you want no sound.

- You also need to press down firmly enough to mute the string but not so firmly that you create a rhythmic click. Creating a rhythmic click is often used in slap (and fingerstyle) and funk lines and is called an open string hammer-on.

- Your muting fingers need to mute the note EXACTLY on beat 2 or 4. You have to aim for this in precisely the same way you would if you were playing a note.

You will often encounter passages in bass lines where you play a higher open string and then play a lower note and have to mute the higher open string to stop it sounding at the same time as the lower note is played, so it's an important technical facility to work on.

Muting System 2 – The Fretting Hand/Fretted Notes

The second muting technique can be a controversial one in bass circles. It's done by playing a fretted note and lifting your finger from the fretboard but still maintaining contact with the string.

Executed correctly this should stop the fretted note from ringing out. But the reason it is a little controversial is that it causes a soft, rhythmic click. There are players who consider this rhythmic click to be an unwelcome by-product of this technique and that it makes your sound a little 'dirty' or messy.

My take on this is that in a band scenario the soft click that this method gives off is virtually impossible to hear. The frequencies that the hi-hats and cymbals are in will disguise this. So it's a valid technique in my opinion.

The bass playing situation where you might want to get rid of this is if you are doing a lot of high level recording.

Here's an example with the quarter notes played at the 5th fret of the E string (so we're playing an 'A' note) and this time the arrows on Beats 2 and 4 go upwards to signify lifting the fingers upwards:

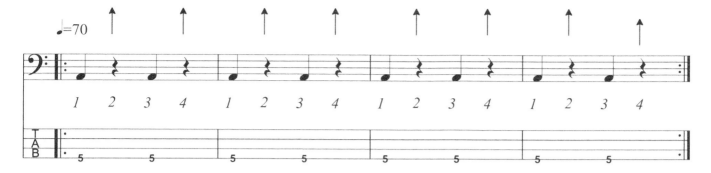

Playing Note: *when using this kind of muting system to create rests I will often bring up the fretting hand finger that is fretting the note and simultaneously lay all the fingers of my fretting hand on the string. This doesn't prevent the rhythmic click but it totally avoids any accidental harmonics which you'll get at specific points of the fretboard.*

Muting System 3 – The Plucking Hand/Open Or Fretted Notes

This is the advanced system that I was talking about – I agonized over whether to even mention it but thought that it deserved mention. What's important to know is that there are multiple variations of this muting system – Gary Willis has his own version, as does Todd Johnson. And there are others too.

So if you come to check this out further on in your playing journey there are several options available.

Essentially in this example the muting is done by a finger of the plucking hand. So in the notation I've replaced the counting of the beat with 'i' and 'm' notations to represent the index and middle fingers:

The challenge of this technique is you need to adapt your existing technique so that instead of plucking, when you mute a note your finger must come to rest on the string being played. This works for either fretted notes or open strings by the way.

I'll demonstrate it in a video on the online version of the Module 1.29 page...but as noted before, we won't be using this again in the HTPB#50 course.

Action Steps

The two techniques I want you to practice for this module are Muting System 1 and 2.

Start – as always – out of tempo and with no tempo reference. And get your hands used to the demands being asked of it.

Only when you've done this several times do you introduce tempo. Select an 8 bar quarter note groove – slowest tempo! – and practice Exercises 1 and 2.

Of course you can transfer Exercises 1 and 2 to other strings – and you should – but I've left that out of this Unit for brevity. Focus on the concept of 'playing the rest' and making your rests start as precisely as you would play a note, and last for precisely a beat.

Module 1.30 Fretboard Mastery 3

In Module 1.22 we started learning the fretboard by focusing on the note E and playing it in every location on the bass.

In the overview video that went with Module 1.22, I also talked through some 'patterns' that you'll find that occur on the bass guitar fretboard due to the way it is tuned. Specifically:

- The double dot at the 12th fret represents the same notes as occur at the nut (i.e. the open strings) – only an octave above. And the arrangement that occurs from frets 0 to 11 repeats on each string starting at fret 12 marked with the double dot.

- By playing two frets higher and two strings higher you'll also get a repeat of a note but an octave higher.

- By playing one string higher BUT five frets back you'll get another iteration of a note.

So bearing these in mind – and cross reference with the video too – if I tell you that the third note we are going to look at is F#, and that the lowest occurrence of that note is at the second fret of the E string, you can already make some inferences about where other F# notes will occur:

- Two frets beyond the 12th fret of the E string will be an F# – an octave higher than the first note (so played at E14).

- Two frets above the 2nd fret and two strings above will be F# – also an octave higher (so played at D4).

- If the 14th fret of the E string is an F#, then if we move up a string and count back 5 frets we'll also get an F#. This is the 9th fret of the A string.

- We can get an octave of *that* note by going up two strings and two frets – so from A9 to G11.

Once you know how symmetrical the bass fretboard is it makes the job of learning the fretboard much easier. To summarize, here are the locations of F# on the various strings:

- E String – 2nd fret and 14th fret
- A String – 9th fret and 21st fret
- D String – 4th fret and 16th fret
- G String – 11th fret and 23rd fret

If you have Precision bass – or a bass modeled on the Precision – you won't be able to hit that note at the 23rd fret of the G string because the Precision only has 21 frets! So here's the ascending exercise finding all the F# notes noted out for a Precision style bass, if your bass has F# at the 23rd fret of the G string, then add it into the exercise:

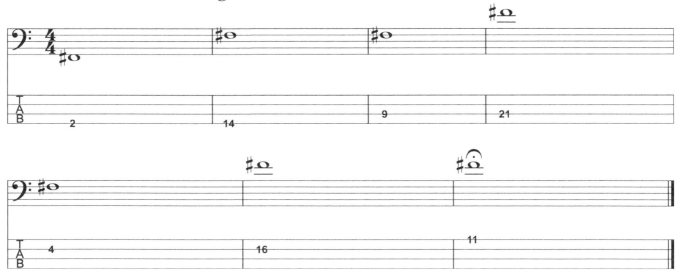

Again notice that you start at the lowest appearance of this note on the E string, and then play the next 'F#' note on the E string. And then move to the A string and play the lowest 'F#' note on the A string….and so on.

When you're comfortable with the locations, then reverse the direction and start with the highest 'F#' on the G String. (If your bass has a high F# at the 23rd fret of the G string, then insert high 'F#' into this exercise):

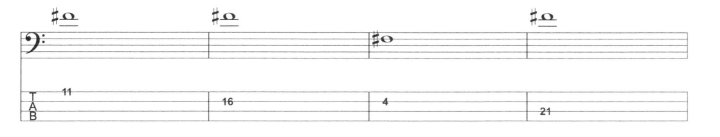

Remember that these exercises are to be played slowly and out of time – and make sure you say 'F#' to yourself every time you play an F#.

I've also prepared a 'fretboard chart' that you can print out which shows all of the note locations for 'F#' on a simulation of a fretboard layout. (Forgive the relatively primitive nature of this – my Photoshop skills are not the best in the world). You'll find that in the PDF on the online Module 1.30 page.

Module 1.31 Song#6 Love Me Don't

Song 6 uses predominantly roots and fifths, in combination with the quarter note/quarter note rest rhythm introduced in Module 1.29. This practice song will be a test of your fretting hand muting. This practice song is a mid-tempo, early Beatles style practice song.

The practice song starts out with an 8 bar intro:

The intro then leads to a verse. This is a 9 bar section which ends on a 'hit' or 'stab' that plays C. There is then a 4 bar transition between the verse and the bridge, making this a 13 bar section:

The bridge is an 8 bar section:

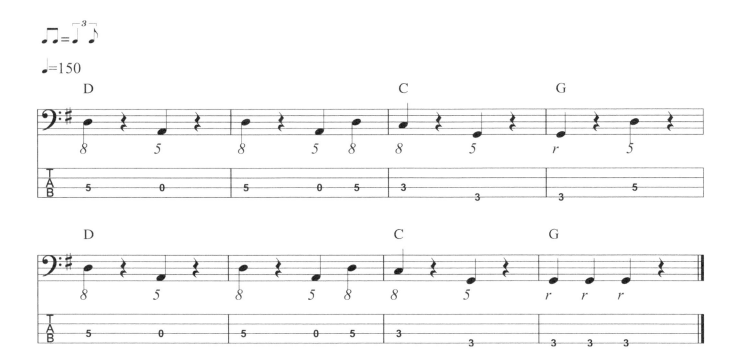

To end the song is another verse which has an outro tag on it. This outro tag is bookended by the 'Start Repeat' and 'End Repeat' markings which you can see at the start and end of the last four bars of this section:

On the website version of Module 1.31 you'll find a PDF with the song sections arranged together that you can print out and place on your music stand for practice and playing purposes.

Additionally there are playalongs of the complete song at different tempo levels, which puts the song sections together like this:

- Intro
- Verse 1
- Bridge
- Verse 2/Outro
- Song finishes on a sustained G chord, so hold a G note

Module 1.32 Song#7 Blue River

Song 7 uses predominantly roots and fifths, in combination with the quarter note/quarter note rest rhythm introduced in Module 1.29. This practice song will be a test of your fretting hand muting. This practice song is a mid-tempo, Creedence style, country-rock practice song.

The practice piece starts out with an 8 bar intro - but the bass doesn't come in until bar 5:

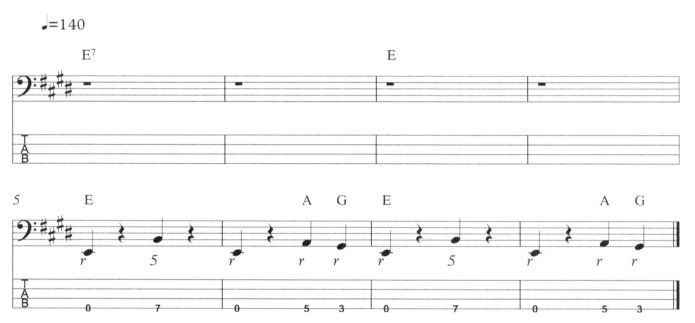

The intro then leads to a verse. This is a 16 bar section where the bass line for the first 8 bars is similar to the last four bars of the intro. So if you've already learned that, you've already got half of the verse under your fingers:

Verse 2 is the next section, this has the same chord structure as Verse 1, but the bass line has some variations when compared with Verse 1:

Module 1.32 135

The practice song finishes with an 8 bar section repeated twice which is based on the main two bar idea. The repeat is instructed by the 'Start Repeat' and 'End Repeat' markings, which you can see at the start, and the end of bar 8 of this section:

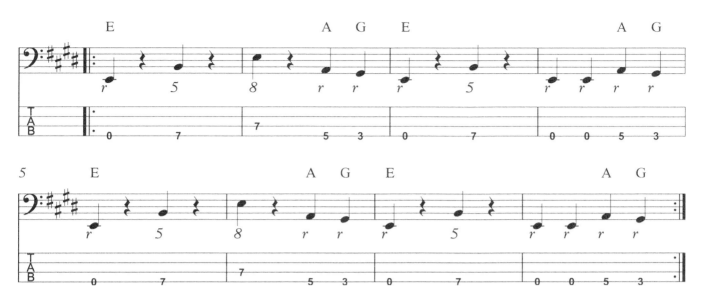

On the website version of Module 1.32 you'll find a PDF with the song sections arranged together that you can print out and place on your music stand for practice and playing purposes.

Additionally there are playalongs of the complete song at different tempo levels, which puts the song sections together like this:

- Intro (bass in at bar 5)
- Verse 1
- Verse 2
- Outro
- Song finishes on an E chord, so play a sustained E

Module 1.33 Fretboard Mastery 4

In Module 1.22 we started learning the fretboard by focusing on the note E and playing it in every location on the bass.

In the overview video that went with Module 1.22, I also talked through some 'patterns' that you'll find that occur on the bass guitar fretboard due to the way it is tuned. Specifically:

- The double dot at the 12th fret represents the same notes as occur at the nut (i.e. the open strings) – only an octave above. And the arrangement that occurs from frets 0 to 11 repeats on each string starting at fret 12 marked with the double dot.

- By playing two frets higher and two strings higher you'll also get a repeat of a note but an octave higher.

- By playing one string higher BUT five frets back you'll get another iteration of a note.

So bearing these in mind – and cross reference with the video too – if I tell you that the fourth note we are going to look at is G and that the lowest occurrence of that note is at the third fret of the E string you can already make some inferences about where other G notes will occur:

- Three frets beyond the 12th fret of the E string will be an G – an octave higher than the first note. That's the fifteenth fret of the E string.

- Two frets above the 3rd fret and two strings above will be G – also an octave higher (so played at D5).

- If the 15th fret of the E string is a G, then if we move up a string and count back 5 frets we'll also get an G. This is the 10th fret of the A string.

- We can get an octave of THAT note by going up two strings and two frets – so from A10 to G12.

- From the G at the 10th fret of the A string, we can move up a string and count back 5 frets...that takes us to D5.

Once you know how symmetrical the bass fretboard is it makes the job of learning the fretboard much easier. To summarize, here are the locations of G on the various strings:

- E String – 3rd fret and 15th fret

- A String – 10th fret and 22nd fret

- D String – 5th fret and 17th fret

- G String – Open String, 12th fret and 24th fret

If you have Precision bass – or a bass modelled on the Precision – you won't be able to hit notes above the 21st fret because the Precision only has 21 frets

Here's the ascending exercise finding all the G notes noted out for 21 Fret basses. If your bass has G at the 22nd fret of the A string, then add it into the exercise and also if you have a 24 fret bass then add in the G at the 24th fret of the G string:

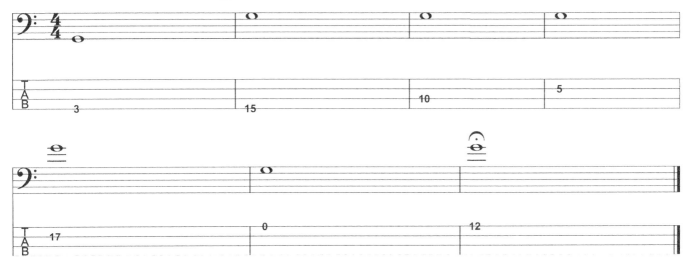

Module 1.33

Again notice that you start at the lowest occurrence of this note on the E string, and then play the next 'G' note on the E string. And then move to the A string and play the lowest 'G' note on the A string….and so on.

When you're comfortable with the locations, then reverse the direction and start with the highest 'G' on the G String:

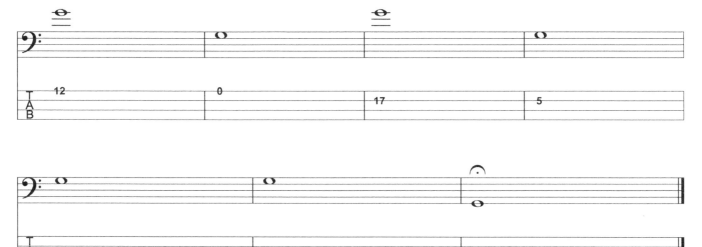

Remember that these exercises are to be played slowly and out of time – and make sure you say 'G' to yourself every time you play a G.

I've also prepared a 'fretboard chart' that you can print out which shows all of the note locations for 'G on a simulation of a fretboard layout. (Forgive the relatively primitive nature of this – my Photoshop skills are not the best in the world). You'll find that in the PDF download on the online version of the Module 1.33 page.

Module 1.34 Song#8 Country Two Beat Blues

Song #8 is the kind of upbeat, vaguely country, two beat blues that you'll find in the discography of Johnny Cash. Tunes like Folsom Prison Blues, Cry Cry Cry, I Walk The Line and others have a distinct feel that we're modelling in this practice song.

There are two verses to this practice song and they are almost identical. The second verse has got a two bar tag, plus a return to the E chord (not shown) to close the song out.

The practice song is played at a tempo of 205 BPM, but the majority of the bass line is composed of quarter notes followed by quarter note rests. So it shouldn't be taxing for your plucking hand.

The bass line is composed of roots and fifths. But note that a two bar idea is created by playing the root and fifth in one bar followed by the octave and fifth in the second bar. There will be more of these combinations when we look at Device 4 in Module 2.

On the following two pages are the notation and tab for the first verse and the second verse:

VERSE 1

VERSE 2

Module 1.34

On the website version of Module 1.34 you'll find a PDF containing the two verses that you can print out and place on your music stand for practice and playing purposes.

Additionally there are playalongs of the complete song at different tempo levels, which puts the song sections together like this:

- Verse 1
- Verse 2

Module 1.35 Creating A Dynamic Practice Schedule

Everyone "knows" that to get better you've got to practice. But not all practice is created equally. Some practice leads to improvement. Some practice leads to no improvement. The purpose of creating a practice schedule is to ensure that as much of your practice as possible is the kind of practice that leads to improvement.

Here is a list of the elements that go into making a successful practice schedule:

- Knowing what you are going to practice.

- Knowing what you are trying to achieve with your practice.

- Weekly and daily practice sheets.

- A digital timer plus everything you need to practice with (e.g. MP3 practice tracks or Band In A Box files) loaded and ready to go.

- Any music/exercises you need printed out and on your music stand.

- A short warm up routine, and if you can make this a learning activity and make it do double duty all the better.

Please note, *Deliberate Practice For Bass* goes into what's needed for successful practice in much more detail.

1. *Knowing What You Are Going To Practice*

There's an old adage that says failure to prepare is preparing to fail. And there's a great element of truth to this - especially for practicing.

If you arrive at your practice area with a finite amount of time available, and have to plan what you are going to practice AND get any practice tracks or music necessary for that practice...then even if that only takes

5 minutes not only have you taken 5 minutes out of your practice when you could have been warming up, but you have also used up some of your energy on planning.

The more tired the brain gets, the less effective your practice becomes. So you need to hoard that brain energy as much as possible because once fatigue sets in effective practice becomes difficult to sustain.

There's another reason though why you need to know what you are going to practice, and prepare a practice routine prior to actually practicing. And that's to ensure that your practice is not only geared towards making you a better player, but is also aligned with what you are actually trying to achieve on the bass. That's the next point.

2. *Knowing What You Are Trying To Achieve With Your Practice*

Now all of the students on the How To Play Bass In 50 Songs are heading towards a point where they will have acquired the following skills:

- Fretting Hand Technique (Double Bass fingering and Finger Per Fret fingering.

- Plucking Hand Technique - two finger rest stroke.

- Fretboard mastery.

- Working knowledge of rhythms down to the 8th note subdivision (that's covered more fully, starting from Module 2).

- Practical applications and developments of the above items via learning and playing the practice songs which are based on real world chord progressions.

Now I've laid these 'goals' out and hardwired them into the DNA of the HTPB 50 Songs learning programme. What's important to look for as the course unfolds, is to see how many exercises I ask you to practice that don't lead towards achieving the above goals. If I do my job correctly you won't find any.

This is important because when you complete the HTPB50 Songs course I want you to take the methodologies that you'll be familiar with and employ them in your continuing development beyond the 5 modules of this course.

The biggest benefit of knowing what you want to achieve on the bass is this: it can be used as a lens to hold your practice schedule to. Anything that doesn't move you forward on your chosen path should be ruthlessly discarded. And you should focus ONLY on practice that moves you forward towards your stated goals.

Note: *bass playing is a part of your life and it's highly likely that, over time, your bass playing goals will change. Maybe you'll decide that you want to play blues rock like Tommy Shannon with Stevie Ray Vaughan. Or fingerstyle funk like Rocco Prestia with Tower of Power. Or walking bass style jazz. The kind of exercises you would practice in each of those instances are different - but if you decided that one of those was what you wanted to do, then assuming you have the basics down (which you'll get from following the How To Play Bass #50 Course) then it's a reasonably simple job to map out the kind of activities that you would need to practice.*

3. Weekly And Daily Practice Sheets

At the end of one practice week, which of course coincides with the start of the next practice week, it's productive to review how your previous week's practice has played out, and plan your upcoming practice week.

This is part of the process of ensuring that your practice schedule is dynamic.

As well as your weekly practice sheet, you'll also need daily practice sheets for the days that you have allocated to practice.

These daily practice sheets should contain the following information:

- The exercises that you are going to practice.

- The precise length of time that you are going to practice for each exercise.

- Suggested tempo levels for each exercise.

- A box to write in how long you actually played the exercise for

- A box to tally the amount of time practiced for the day.

Ideally you'll also have a file or binder to file these daily and weekly practice sheets into. As the file grows in your practice space, the accumulation of pages will help with generating momentum and keep up your practicing habit going.

4. *A Digital Timer And Everything You Need Pre-Programmed And Ready To Go*

Any preparation of practice tracks you need for your practice should be done *before* practicing. Preferably the day before.

When you come to practice for the day, all the tracks you need should be lined up and ready to go, so that you only have to hit 'OPEN SONG' on your Band In A Box program - or cue up a drum track from your computer or smart device. That prevents practice erosion and allows you to switch from one exercise to the next with the minimum of time necessary.

If you diligently track every exercise and how long you practiced it for - that's what the digital timer is for - and only record *that* as practice time on your practice sheets then you can keep an accurate tally of the actual time you spent practicing. And not include time spent on looking for practice tracks, or tuning.

5. *Any Music You Need Printed Out And Ready To Go On Your Music Stand*

This is an offshoot of the previous section. But it's worth emphasizing this point and giving it its own paragraph. And of course it also ties into #1 above too - if you *know* what you are going to be practicing before you even go to your practice space, then that makes the job of getting the practice actually done just that little bit easier. (There are some days where making practicing even tiny percentages easier makes the probability of getting started and finishing your practice session much higher).

So any exercises or music that you need for your practice session need to be printed out and on your music stand. Or if you use a computer to display your music or an iPad, you need to have that ready to go.

6. *A Short Warm Up Routine*

The warm up routine serves three vital practice functions:

- It warms the hands up. So for this you only need to play something that's slow and easy.

- It kick starts the practice session and creates practice momentum. If you know that the very first exercise is going to be easy then there's less mental resistance to getting started. Being able to quickly tick off the first exercise on your practice sheet gives your practice session early momentum.

- If you can make your warm up exercise ALSO do double duty and be something that moves you forward on the bass guitar, then that's a two for the price of one kind of deal.

Exercises that you can use to warm up that could contribute to your improvement as a bass player include:

- Fretboard Mastery exercises.

- Fretting hand exercises. These should be done in whole notes at around 50 or 60 BPM. So they can be used as warm ups.

- Slow sections of song - if you're learning a complex song and are learning it by chunking it down and slowing it right down, you can use these sections played really slowly to warm up on.

Making Starting Your Practice As Frictionless As Possible

Even though you have your practice session planned out, your music is printed, your MP3 files are cued up and so on, there are still small obstacles in the way of your practice session.

The ideal is that you have set aside say an hour at 5 pm for practicing and at 5 pm you start practicing. Anything that delays or stops you from practicing at your appointed time has got the possibility to derail your entire practice session. I've created several "pre-practice" habits designed to avoid this. So that if I'm scheduled to practice at 5 pm I can be confident that I will practice at 5 pm.

Here are my "pre-practice" habits.

(i) The bass I'm going to use is on a stand in my practice space and is ready to go. (Advantage of this is that if you get say 10 minutes where you are waiting for a phone call and have nothing to do, you can pick the bass up and do something constructive for 10 minutes - obviously if you're not self employed this is harder). Ideally you want to be able to pick up your bass, check the tuning, plug in and start practicing.

(ii) The computer - if, like me, you use it to help with practice - is already booted up and any programmes needed are running.

(iii) Drinks and refreshments are to hand and anything that might make you put your bass down (like go to the toilet) has been done.

(iv) Mobile Phones and Email Programmes are switched off. If you practice at a set time each day make sure your friends and family know, and that they know that if they call you they'll get voicemail.

(v) Some of this can be done concurrently - if your computer is not switched on, then switch it on, and whilst it's booting you can go grab a cup of coffee. Once it's booted and you've logged in then you can grab your bass, quickly check the tuning, look at your first practice sheet, program your digital timer and your pretty close to being ready to warm up.

If you don't use anything from the computer as a metronome - and you need a metronome for your warm up exercise - you can even do your warm up whilst the computer is booting up.

For a few days keep a log of anything that you "have to" do before practicing - and see if you can find any patterns. If so, then try and set up pre-practice routines so that these activities don't make the job of moving from not practicing to practicing harder.

The reason for all this: sometimes you're not in the mood to practice and it won't take much to dissuade you. If on the other hand getting started is pretty easy then you can just make a deal with yourself: I'll do 10 minutes and then call it a day.

On these kind of days getting that first 10 minutes under your belt is often all that's needed for you to go on successfully complete your practice session.

How To Make Your Practice Sessions Dynamic

One of the reasons why writing down practice tempos is so important is that it directly leads into the most important thing about practice sessions - and that's making them dynamic.

Now in this context dynamic simply means that they change over time.

It's also important because when you practice the same things over and over and over you won't get any better. To keep making improvements your practice has to change to reflect the growth in your playing abilities that comes from the practice you do.

Let me give you a practical example of this. Let's say you are working on your two fingered rest stroke, and are practicing single string exercises in quarter notes. And you practice leading with the index finger and then strictly alternating, and leading with the middle finger and strictly alternating.

Now if you play these exercises for 10 minutes every day at 60 BPM - and keep it at 60 BPM, what will happen is that the exercise will become comfortable reasonably quickly and once that happens you will be getting little benefit from continue to practice these exercises at 60 BPM.

But if you make a note that the exercise is comfortable on your daily practice sheet, and then when you next come to play this exercise you move the tempo to 70 BPM....now you'll find that the exercise becomes challenging again. Which means that you are working on improvement.

Over time you should see a steady upward climb in tempos that matches the improvement in your abilities and it's directly correlated to the practice that you've been putting in.

That's a simple description of the difference between a static practice schedule and a dynamic practice schedule. When you extend this concept to just about every single exercise in your practice schedule - so that your exercise tempos creep up slowly but steadily over time - then you can't help but improve.

Tracking the tempo levels from day to day - and during a weekly review - allows you to be consistently making sure that you are pushing forward all the time. Improvement is rarely made from giant leaps forward, but nearly always from an accumulation of small increments. Not only can you now track these increments, but you can also systematically increase them and be 100% confident that you are working on incremental improvement in a deliberate and purposeful fashion.

One Final Thing To Note

There's another task that you need to put in your weekly review. And it's highly important in your long term development as a bass player.

This task is to go through your daily practice sheets for the week, review ALL of the exercises you have recorded on those sheets and ask this question of EVERY exercise:

> *Is this exercise leading me forwards to my bass goals?*

For the How To Play Bass in 50 Songs course all the suggested exercises built into the course are designed to improve your skills in the following foundational areas:

- Fretting hand technique.
- Plucking hand technique.
- Fretboard knowledge.
- Rhythmic knowledge.
- Practical combinations of the above using practice songs.

When you get beyond the 5 modules of this course though, it's important to make this a regular part of your weekly review and to ensure you don't get sidetracked.

Summary

We've covered a lot of ground in this Unit. In some ways this Unit is a 10 page snapshot of my book ***Deliberate Practice For Bass***. There is much more detail in there on what it takes in order to get the most out of your practice.

The main takeaways of this unit are:

(i) Prepare your practice in advance - failing to prepare IS preparing to fail.

(ii) Remove distractions (e.g. phones and email programs). They can wait.

(iii) Time every exercise religiously. And record those times on your daily practice sheets. This is the only way to know exactly how much practice you are doing.

(iv) Prepare weekly and daily practice schedules in advance so that the minute you get to your practice session you can focus on exactly you have to do simply by looking at your daily sheet for the upcoming practice session.

(v) All practice activities should contribute towards you achieving your bass goal. If it doesn't, strike it. No matter how rich you are, time is an asset that once you've spent it you can't get back.

(vi) File your weekly and daily sheets in a practice binder. As it fills up with practice sheets it generates its own momentum and helps with getting you to practice on those days when you don't feel like it.

End Note

Most bass players practice in a manner that I call "Random Practice." Random Practice isn't designed and leads to either random improvement or zero improvement. Focused practice is much more effective and delivers much better results.

In the long term, just two 15 minute sessions of focused practice a day, repeated on a consistent basis through a practice week, will deliver more results than several hour of random practice per week.

So build a system to maximize and optimize your practice sessions in order to make constant and consistent improvement and grow as a bass player.

Module 1.36 Module 1 Checklist And Guidelines

Another useful way to track and monitor your progress is to check off the individual units in Module 1 and tick them off as completed. Each unit is listed again here. As well as the unit name, and a checkbox, there is also a summary of practice tempos to be achieved in order to tick the exercise off.

Put a tick in the checkbox when you're happy with your progress for that unit.

Module 1.1 The Two Finger Rest Stroke ☐

Module 1.1 lays out the basic set up of the plucking hand for the two finger rest stroke. The important things to note are the changing position of the thumb depending on which string you're plucking, and the angle of the plucking hand arm.

Module 1.2 Plucking Hand 1 ☐

Module 1.2 features two whole note plucking hand exercises on the open E string. Suggested tempo levels range from 60 to 100 BPM. Be confident of playing these exercises at least at 80 BPM before proceeding.

Module 1.3 Plucking Hand 2 ☐

Module 1.3 features whole note plucking hand exercises on the remaining open strings. Suggested tempo levels range from 60 to 100 BPM. Be confident of playing these exercises at least at 80 BPM before proceeding.

Module 1.4 Plucking Hand 3 ☐

Module 1.4 features two half note plucking hand exercises on the open E string. Suggested tempo levels range from 60 to 100 BPM. Be confident of playing these exercises at least at 80 BPM before proceeding.

Module 1.5 Plucking Hand 4 ☐

Module 1.5 features half note plucking hand exercises on the remaining open strings. Suggested tempo levels range from 60 to 100 BPM. Be confident of playing these exercises at least at 80 BPM before proceeding.

Module 1.6 Fretting Hand - Double Bass Fingering ☐

Module 1.6 is the first fretting hand Unit. There are two videos to watch and a slow, fretting hand exercise to add to your daily practice.

Module 1.7 Fretting Hand - One Finger Per Fret ☐

Module 1.7 is the second fretting hand Unit. There are two videos to watch and a slow, fretting hand exercise to add to your daily practice.

Module 1.8 What Is An 80-20 Bass Device? ☐

Module 1.8 is a 'read-only' unit and introduces the concept of an 80-20 Bass Device. read the Unit, watch the videos, and make sure you have a grasp of the concept.

Module 1.9 Device 1 The Root Note ☐

Module 1.9 has got two half note practice exercises using the root note with different chord progressions. Make sure you can play those practice exercises at 80 BPM at least. Strive for 100 BPM.

Module 1.10 Song#1 "Don't Imagine" ☐

Module 1.10 introduces the first practice song. There are downloadable tracks for both the song chunks and the complete song to download and practice with. The recommended 'performance tempo' is 80 BPM. So that's the goal for this Unit.

Module 1.11 Plucking Hand 5 ☐

Module 1.11 introduces string crossing plucking hand exercises with a whole note rhythm. Start out slowly, but you should be aiming for a guide tempo of 100 BPM for the 4 exercises in the book and the two bonus exercises on the online Module 1.11 page.

Module 1.12 Plucking Hand 6 ☐

Module 1.12 introduces string crossing plucking hand exercises with a half note rhythm. Start out slowly, but you should be aiming for a guide tempo of 100 BPM for the 4 exercises in the book and the two bonus exercises on the online Module 1.12 page.

Module 1.13 Plucking Hand 7 ☐

Module 1.13 continues string crossing plucking hand exercises with a whole note rhythm. Start out slowly, but you should be aiming for a guide tempo of 100 BPM for the 4 exercises in the book and the two bonus exercises on the online Module 1.13 page.

Module 1.14 Plucking Hand 8 ☐

Module 1.14 introduces string crossing plucking hand exercises with a half note rhythm. Start out slowly, but you should be aiming for a guide tempo of 100 BPM for the 4 exercises in the book and the two bonus exercises on the online Module 1.14 page.

Module 1.15 Song#2 "Have I Told You Recently" ☐

Module 1.15 introduces the second practice song. There are downloadable tracks for both the song chunks and the complete song to download and practice with. The recommended 'performance tempo' is 80 BPM. So that's the goal for this Unit.

Module 1.16 Plucking Hand 9 ☐

Module 1.16 introduces string crossing plucking hand exercises with a half note rhythm. Start out slowly, but you should be aiming for a guide tempo of 100 BPM for the 4 exercises in the book and the two bonus exercises on the online Module 1.16 page.

Module 1.17 Song#3 "Hey John" ☐

Module 1.17 introduces the third practice song. There are downloadable tracks for both the song chunks and the complete song to download and practice with. The recommended 'performance tempo' is 80 BPM. So that's the goal for this Unit.

Module 1.18 Plucking Hand 10 ☐

Module 1.18 introduces string crossing plucking hand exercises with a quarter note rhythm. Start out slowly, but you should be aiming for a guide tempo of at least 80 BPM for the 4 exercises in the book, and the two bonus exercises on the online Module 1.18 page

Module 1.19 Song #4 "Every Country Breath You Take" ☐

Module 1.19 introduces the fourth practice song. There are downloadable tracks for both the song chunks and the complete song to download and practice with. The recommended 'performance tempo' is 100 BPM. So that's the goal for this Unit.

Module 1.20 Plucking Hand 11

Module 1.20 consists of quarter note plucking hand exercises that play all four open strings. The guide tempo to aim for is 80 BPM, but if you can push to 100 BPM that could be thought of as a 'stretch goal' - that's explicitly targeted in Module 1.23!

Module 1.21 Device 2 - The 5th

Module 1.21 introduces the second 80-20 Bass device. There are some quarter note practice exercises to get you started with root and 5ths. The guide tempo to aim for is 80 BPM, but if you can push to 100 BPM that could be thought of as a 'stretch goal.'

Module 1.22 Fretboard Mastery 1

Module 1.22 introduces the first fretboard mastery exercise, to learn the note 'E' everywhere it occurs on the fretboard. There are no tempo guidelines for this exercise, just playing it slowly and accurately is more important. This can serve as a warm up exercise. (See the notes in Module 1.35 for more on this).

Module 1.23 Plucking Hand 12

Module 1.23 consists of quarter note plucking hand exercises that play all four open strings. The guide tempo to aim for is 100 BPM.

Module 1.24 Fretting Hand 3

Module 1.24 is the third fretting hand Unit. There is an overview videos to watch and a slow, fretting hand exercise to add to your daily practice. See Module 1.35 for using these exercises as warm ups.

Module 1.25 Fretting Hand 4 ☐

Module 1.24 is the fourth fretting hand Unit. There are two slow, fretting hand exercise to add to your daily practice. See Module 1.35 for using these exercises as warm ups.

Module 1.26 Fretboard Mastery 2 ☐

Module 1.26 introduces the second fretboard mastery exercise, to learn the note 'F' everywhere it occurs on the fretboard. There are no tempo guidelines for this exercise, just playing it slowly and accurately is more important. This can serve as a warm up exercise. (See the notes in Module 1.35 for more on this).

Module 1.27 More Practice With The 5th ☐

In Module 1.27 there are further exercises with the second 80-20 Bass device - which is the root and 5th. The guide tempo to aim for is 80 BPM - these exercises are designed for increasing fretboard knowledge combined with device knowledge rather than focusing on technical facility.

Module 1.28 Song#5 "Bad Moon Falling" ☐

Module 1.28 introduces the fifth practice song. There are downloadable tracks for both the song chunks and the complete song to download and practice with. The recommended 'performance tempo' is 160 BPM. So that's the goal for this Unit. Note that the bass line is in half notes, so this equates to a quarter note line at 80 BPM!

Module 1.29 Quarter Notes With Rests ☐

Module 1.29 consists of quarter note/quarter note rest plucking hand exercises. The guide tempo to aim for is 80 BPM. But if you can push to 100 BPM that could be thought of as a 'stretch goal.'

Module 1.30 Fretboard Mastery 3

☐

Module 1.30 introduces the third fretboard mastery exercise, to learn the note 'F´#' everywhere it occurs on the fretboard. There are no tempo guidelines for this exercise, just playing it slowly and accurately is more important. This can serve as a warm up exercise. (See the notes in Module 1.35 for more on this).

Module 1.31 Song #6 Love Me Don't

☐

Module 1.31 introduces the sixth practice song. There are downloadable tracks for both the song chunks and the complete song to download and practice with. The recommended 'performance tempo' is 150 BPM. So that's the goal for this Unit. Note that the bass line is in quarter notes with quarter note rests, so this equates to a quarter note line at 75 BPM!

Module 1.32 Song#7 Blue River.

☐

Module 1.32 introduces the seventh practice song. There are downloadable tracks for both the song chunks and the complete song to download and practice with. The recommended 'performance tempo' is 140 BPM. So that's the goal for this Unit. Note that the bass line is in quarter notes with quarter note rests, so this equates to a quarter note line at 70 BPM!

Module 1.33 Fretboard Mastery 4

Module 1.33 introduces the fourth fretboard mastery exercise, to learn the note 'G' everywhere it occurs on the fretboard. There are no tempo guidelines for this exercise, just playing it slowly and accurately is more important. This can serve as a warm up exercise. (See the notes in Module 1.35 for more on this).

Module 1.34 Song #8 Country Two Beat Blues

Module 1.34 introduces the eighth practice song. There are downloadable tracks for both the song chunks and the complete song to download and practice with. The recommended 'performance tempo' is 205 BPM. So that's the goal for this Unit. Note that the bass line is essentially half notes, so this equates to a quarter note line at approximately 100 BPM!

Module 1.35 Creating A Dynamic Practice Schedule

In Module 1.35 the concept of creating a dynamic practice schedule is introduced. This is a process that I highly recommend so read this Unit carefully. As mentioned in the unit itself, this unit is like a 10 page summary of my book *Deliberate Practice For Bass*, so there are further options if you want to dive deeper into this.

Updates, Bonus Lessons, And More...

For updates, tutorials and 80-20 bass themed material you can check out my website:

    www.how-to-play-bass.com

If you've not yet sent an email (with a copy of your Amazon receipt) to get added to the bonus online version of this volume, you can email me directly at:

    paul@how-to-play-bass.com

The online version of the book has got all the filmed examples, practice MP3s to download, bonus lessons and more.

Please note: if there's anything you don't understand, or you spot something you think may be a typo, don't hesitate to use the email address above and drop me an email and ask a question. And don't hesitate to send me a nudge if you've not a reply within 48 hours.

Stay safe, practice hard, practice smart and strive to be the kind of bass player that other musicians want to play with.

Paul Wolfe
SW England

Printed in France by Amazon
Brétigny-sur-Orge, FR